Nostalgic Bolton

To Metta and Alan

from Joan (HUDSON)

July 2009.

This Book
Belongs to
Alan W. Brodrick

The publishers would like to thank the following companies for their

support in the production of this book

Astley Dye & Chemical Co. Ltd

Carrs Pasties

George Cox & Sons Ltd

Gregory & Porritts

House of Raja's

H W Audio Ltd

MBDA UK Ltd

Prestons of Bolton

Rivington Taylor

Russell & Russell Solicitors

T Sutcliffe & Co. Ltd

J Taylor (Electrical Contactors) Ltd

Thomas Harwood

Vernacare

Warburtons

First published in Great Britain by True North Books Limited
England HX3 6AE
01422 344344

ISBN 1 903204 99 2

Text, design and origination by True North Books
Printed and bound by The Amadeus Press

Nostalgic Bolton

CONTENTS

INTRODUCTION

We make no excuses for wallowing in nostalgia, hence the title of this book. It is the latest in a series of True North publications that turn back the pages of time and linger lovingly on places, people and events of yesteryear. Some of them will be familiar to the reader, while others are nearly forgotten and shrouded in the mists of time. Our parents and grandparents may have alluded to still yet more that is now completely eradicated, but form an important part of the heritage that made our town the grand place that we call home.

Max Bygraves was quite right when he sang 'Fings ain't what they used to be'. Can it really be just about half a century ago that we nodded knowingly at some of the lyrics? Yet, his words now seem outdated. He sang of parking meters and bowling alleys as being newfangled items. No doubt in years to come our descendants will smile condescendingly at the antiquated way we drove our cars to get to the shops or used computer keyboards to write letters. 'Nostalgic Bolton' is not a dry and dusty history book, but a celebration of life in the earlier decades of the last century. All the photographs within have been enhanced by the attachment of captions intended to inform or even provoke comment. They are not image titles, but text designed to highlight elements of each picture and, on occasion, offer a pithy outlook on the background or times in which the scenes were observed. Hopefully, this will prompt the reader into reflecting on his or her own interpretation. Feel free to disagree, for then we have succeeded in stimulating discussion. That can only be of benefit as we think back over how life might have been in the times depicted or how it really was if we are old enough to recall those days. Perhaps for some of us those memories have a hazy hue and the photographs will help bring everything flooding back. The camera never lies, though its angles might offer a slightly different perspective.

There really was an age, not too long ago, when the car did not reign supreme and when children played with home made toys without the need of computer chips with everything. People went shopping in the market for fresh fruit and families sat round tables together to eat their evening meals. They listened to the radio, grouped in front of a crackling set that brought 'Dick Barton', 'ITMA' and Henry Hall's orchestra into the front room. Out on the streets rag and bone men called out for business, offering to exchange unwanted household scrap for pegs to be used on the washing line and donkey stones to enhance the appearance of the doorstep.

It is now time to relive those days and turn the first page. Enter a world when a policeman stood on point duty on Bradshawgate and the Tonge Moor tram rattled along as it passed the cobblestones on Nelson Square. Go back to the time when men bought hats at Dunn's and sweethearts went to RG Connor's to buy that engagement ring. Lift a glass of ale bought at Munro's off licence and salute our town, our Bolton.

Last, but by no means least we would like to thank the numerous prominent Bolton companies who have supported the production of this book. Within these pages the story of each of them is told - their own proud histories and prospects for the future adding to the rich tapestry of life in Bolton.

TEXT	ANDREW MITCHELL, STEVE AINSWORTH
PHOTOGRAPH COMPILATION	TONY LAX
DESIGNER	SEAMUS MOLLOY
BUSINESS DEVELOPMENT EDITOR	PETER PREST

This view of Deansgate, taken at the Knowsley Street corner, dates from 1908. It was a time of gas lamps on the pavements and tramtracks on the streets. In the distance, a horse and cart makes its easy paced way towards the camera. On the right hand side, the local newsagent had his billboards propped up outside the shop. How different the important newspaper stories would be when compared with those of a century later. Emmeline Pankhurst was big news. She had spent time in Holloway Prison for obstructing the police as she tried to get over her point to the general public about women's suffrage. Some good news from the government came in the shape of a new benefit, worth five shillings (25p) per week that was to be paid to everyone over the age of 70; everyone that is except for those who had failed to work according to their ability, prisoners, the insane and paupers. London hosted the Olympic Games. In the athletics section there were many events that we still have today. But, there was one contest where we reigned supreme. In the tug of war, Great Britain provided teams that finished first and second.

STREET SCENES

ooking from the Town Hall steps, across to the imposing Gas Offices, this photograph from the early 1920s shows a busy vista. There are a large number of charabancs lined up, so maybe we are looking at the start of a grand day out to celebrate a special occasion. These fine old days of motoring involved bowling along the open road, frightening cows in the fields as you passed by. Individuals sometimes behaved like Mr Toad and deployed the motor horn with gusto, not to mention the accelerator pedal. But, the charabanc driver was more circumspect and acknowledged his responsibilities in transporting his passengers safely on their day trip.

The Market Cross in the centre of Churchgate provides the link with these photographs from 1925 and 1963. The plates and bronze shields around the base contain references to important dates in the town's history. These include 1253, when Bolton was made a Free Borough, 1631 when the population reached the 500 mark, 1828 when the first railway ran from the town and 1901 when the population in the census was recorded in excess of 160,000. George Harwood, Bolton's Member of Parliament from 1895 to 1912, provided the funds for the erection of the replacement Market Cross that was unveiled on 16 October, 1909. Rising 20 feet above its plinth, the edifice was constructed from stone quarried in Devon. The earlier cross, made of gilded iron, was placed here in 1486 but taken down some 300 years later after coachmen raised repeated objections to it as a hazardous obstruction. James, Earl of Derby, had found the Cross worse than just a nuisance. He was executed before it on 15 October, 1651, having been dubiously convicted of treason for supporting the Royalist cause during the English Civil War. John Wesley preached in front of it on 28 August, 1748. However, his brand of religion was not well received and he was stoned and generally abused by the locals who took objection to his criticism of their so-called sinful ways. At least he kept his head.

Right: The bobby on point duty as seen in this 1927 picture, was a familiar sight at busy road junctions for another 40 years, stationed on Deansgate, outside the Midland Bank, he had an important role to fulfil. Standing like a granite effigy on his little plinth, he had the power to bring traffic to a standstill as he imperiously motioned pedestrians across the road. With just one sweep of a white sleeved arm he motioned traffic forward along the street or permitted it to join from the side. Whenever

he pointed at you it was if he was mimicking the famous World War One poster of Lord Kitchener, 'Your country needs you.' He did not need whistles and wild gestures like his continental counterparts. He was calm and, of course, British. At first, point duty was a fairly comfortable if boring job, with little traffic on the streets. However, it became almost a mathematical exercise as the proliferation of motor cars presented the policeman with the need for eyes in the back of his head. He must also have suffered from breathing in the fumes from the exhausts of cars that emitted much more poisonous gases than is allowed today.

Below: Bradshawgate was busy with traffic even in 1936. This was a decade when the government became concerned about road safety. There was plenty of room in both rural and urban areas for occasional cars and lorries in the first quarter of the last century, but as the numbers of vehicles increased dramatically something had to be done to halt the carnage on our roads that gave us one of the worst reputations in Europe. Electrically operated traffic lights were introduced at many town and city centre junctions in the 1930s and Percy Shaw's cats' eyes were a boon to drivers at night, especially in outlying districts. The Highway Code was issued, offering fundamental instruction and advice to road users and, at long last, new drivers were made to take a driving test before being allowed out unaccompanied. The black and white striped beacon on the right of the picture was a piece of 'street furniture' that we still have today. Named after Leslie Hore-Belisha, the Minister for Transport when it was introduced, this beacon and its partner on the other side of the street marked an area that was designated as a crossing place for pedestrians. The black and white road markings that made the crossing easier to spot were not introduced until the early 1950s.

Left: The finest vehicles of their age were lined up on the south side of Victoria Square in June, 1930. Perhaps they belonged to aldermen and council officials going about their work in the Town Hall. The imposing building was rebuilt after a devastating fire on 14 November, 1981. The original Albert Hall was lost, but the rest of the building was, thankfully, saved. The regenerated structure now includes the new Albert Hall and Festival Hall. The foundation stone for the original Town Hall was laid in 1867, though there was no real ceremony held to mark the occasion. Apparently, there was some dispute as to who should have the honour of wielding the ceremonial trowel. As no agreement could be reached, the stone was put in place by an unknown hand without any of the traditional pomp to accompany it. At least the opening of the magnificent building was properly recognised. On 5 June, 1873, Albert, Prince of Wales, accompanied by his wife, Alexandra, presided over the formalities. They would eventually become our King and Queen, with Albert using his second name to reign as Edward VII. The silver key that was used to turn the lock of the great front doors by the Prince of Wales was taken away for safe keeping and can now be seen in Bolton Museum.

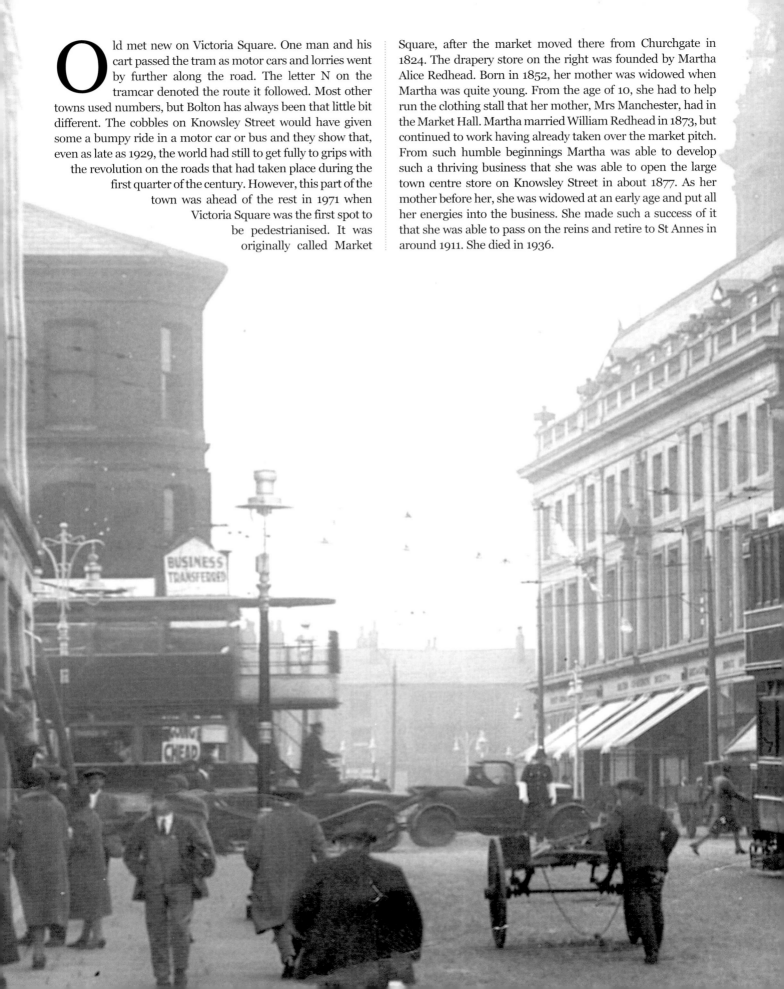

Old met new on Victoria Square. One man and his cart passed the tram as motor cars and lorries went by further along the road. The letter N on the tramcar denoted the route it followed. Most other towns used numbers, but Bolton has always been that little bit different. The cobbles on Knowsley Street would have given some a bumpy ride in a motor car or bus and they show that, even as late as 1929, the world had still to get fully to grips with the revolution on the roads that had taken place during the first quarter of the century. However, this part of the town was ahead of the rest in 1971 when Victoria Square was the first spot to be pedestrianised. It was originally called Market Square, after the market moved there from Churchgate in 1824. The drapery store on the right was founded by Martha Alice Redhead. Born in 1852, her mother was widowed when Martha was quite young. From the age of 10, she had to help run the clothing stall that her mother, Mrs Manchester, had in the Market Hall. Martha married William Redhead in 1873, but continued to work having already taken over the market pitch. From such humble beginnings Martha was able to develop such a thriving business that she was able to open the large town centre store on Knowsley Street in about 1877. As her mother before her, she was widowed at an early age and put all her energies into the business. She made such a success of it that she was able to pass on the reins and retire to St Annes in around 1911. She died in 1936.

Above: Not a car in sight. Now, what would you give for that to be repeated today? Even the trams and the bus appear to be at rest in this peaceful scene and, but for a knot of pedestrians and potential passengers, this would almost appear to be a ghost town. But, as we know, that is far from the truth as Bolton is a busy, vibrant place. Today, its population is almost 140,000, but it is nearly double that when including the satellite boroughs, towns and villages. The most rapid rise occurred during the 19th century as the Industrial Revolution took hold. At the start of the 1800s we had a humble figure of about 17,000 living here. That multiplied 10 fold in just 50 years. Further back in time, Bolton was a small village, referred to by the Saxons as 'Bothi tun', meaning a place with an important building. However, it did not even warrant a mention in the Domesday Book and was not granted the status of a town until 1251.

Below: The view at night along Deansgate, looking towards the Knowsley Street junction and Churchgate, was taken in 1958. On the right is the Westminster Bank at 24 Deansgate, formerly the home of the Bank of Bolton. As we moved towards the end of the 1950s, there was a greater interest in banking for the simple reason that we were beginning to realise that we had more money in our pockets than had been the case for many years. The austere postwar years had finally been left behind and, as Prime Minister Macmillan was happy to tell us, in economic terms, 'we had never had it so good'. Unemployment had fallen and wage packets started to bulge. Our homes suddenly found places for items that once were regarded as luxuries that could only be afforded by the middle classes. A refrigerator meant that housewives could shop less frequently for perishable goods. The twin tub washing machine did away with the washboard, dolly tub and mangle that our parents had used. There was a gleaming 14 inch screen television in the corner of the lounge and conversation the next morning was about life on Emergency Ward 10 rather than what had been occurring in Ambridge. We even had a Ford Popular parked outside the front gate. The bright lights of the town centre mirrored the hopes for a bright future for us all.

Residents of Barchester Avenue, Breightmet, on an estate north of Bury Road, looked very happy in August 1949 as they came out into the street, bathing in the glow of the new sodium lights that lit up the roadway. The first public installation of low pressure sodium light in the UK was on Purley Way, in Croydon, in December 1932. This location was chosen simply because it was just outside the Philips factory where lamps were manufactured. The design of the lamp did not change significantly between the early 1930s and 1955, but later types were introduced that shone more brightly and lasted longer before burning out. Breightmet means 'bright meadow'.

Above: Newport Street on a rainy day in December 1955 was a gloomy sight. Viewed from the southern part across Great Moor Street junction, looking towards the Town Hall, the scene matches some of the national feelings of the time. It was now a decade since we had won the war, but we were hardly living in a land of plenty. Although rationing had ended, at long last, in the previous year, the housewife's purse was hardly bursting with spare cash. It was not quite the grim austerity of the late 40s and early 50s, but we did not feel as if we were living in a land of milk and honey just yet. There was also trouble brewing overseas. The Communist Bloc was strengthened by the signing of the Warsaw Pact and the cold war threatened to spill over into something uncomfortably warmer. At home, there was little to cheer about. Poor Princess Margaret had to say goodbye to the man she loved, the Home Secretary refused to grant a reprieve to Ruth Ellis for killing her wayward boyfriend and allowed her hanging to go ahead and purchase tax, post and phone charges all rose in the autumn budget. To make matters worse, the BBC killed off Grace Archer in a stable fire just because ITV was launched.

Below: Although the incursion of water into homes and businesses damages property and possessions, it is the aftermath that is even worse. The cleaning up operation is as prolonged as the stench that accompanies each occurrence. After any flood there is also a real danger of disease. Children are prone to splash around in the filthy water that gathers in the street, thinking it a lark, oblivious to the dangers of what germs and bacteria lie within those murky depths. This elderly resident, watched by a couple of her neighbours, shovelled away some of the mud that had been brought into her house on Wolfenden Street by the floods of July 1969. Alice Heyes knew that her carpets and lino were probably ruined forever, but she stretched them out on the pavement to dry, just in case something could be salvaged. Hopefully, she had insurance, but not everyone felt as if it could be afforded. At least the residents on the street were friendly and neighbourly, as was often the case in working class communities who lived in the traditional terraced properties. They would chip in with some meaningful contributions where they could.

Left: Magee and Marshall's Crown Works was just one of many smaller breweries that operated successfully in the earlier 20th century before the beer trade fell into the hands of the giants. Some were taken over, others just disappeared. It was a sign of the times, because the same thing happened on the High Streets of Britain as the supermarkets, brought to the demise of many small traders. Just as with food, the taste of the modern product was never the same. The individuality of the small brewer's amber nectar was lost. Those of us who have lived and drunk our way though the changes will recall the days in the middle of the last century when pressurised keg beers first appeared. Is it any wonder that Camra came into being and that Black Sheep and others like it are now sought out by discerning quaffers?

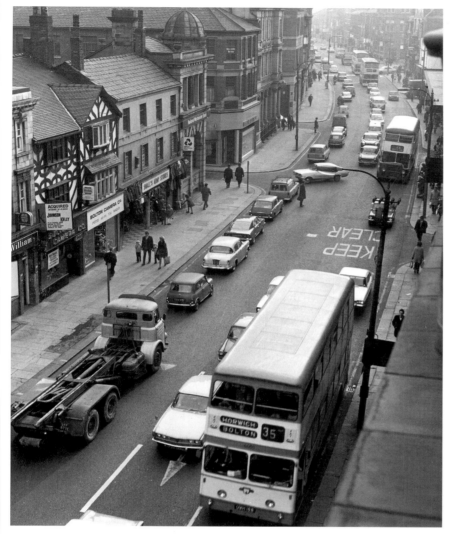

had to be a shepherd again was mystifying. Surely as a top infant he could have risen to the dizzy heights of being a king instead of having to wear that striped tea towel once more. At least Anne had a speaking part in the juniors' version of 'Babushka'. As we popped in and out of the shops, the strains of 'Have yourself a merry little Christmas' became intermingled with 'Ernie, the fastest milkman in the west' over the loudspeakers. Only a week to go, thank goodness.

Below: This part of Newport Street, leading into Victoria Square, is now pedestrianised. The Ford Anglias on view give the photograph a definite 1960s feel. This car was one of the most popular small family saloons to be seen on our roads in those days. The 105E model was first manufactured in 1959 at around the same time that the Mini and the Triumph Herald made their bows. Its distinctive styling made it one of the icons of the era and in continued in production until 1967. Ford had finally seen sense and ditched the pre-war designed sidevalve engine and replaced it with an overhead valve 997cc unit, mated to a new four speed gearbox. Its reverse slope rear window and pointed fins make it instantly recognisable even now. Over 1 million were produced before it was replaced by the Ford Escort, though this retained many of the under the bonnet features of its predecessor.

Left and above: Bradshawgate was busy with Saturday shoppers in the run up to Christmas in 1971. There was just one week to go and it was getting close to the time when last minute panic would be setting in. Was that 14 lb turkey we ordered at the butcher's really big enough to feed the family and grandpa, grandma, Uncle Len and his latest fancy woman as well? Thoughts went back to last year when we realised that cousin Flo had been missed off the Christmas card list and how miffed she was. Did we remember this year? It is hard to recall as they were posted over a week ago to beat the GPO deadline. Well, it was too late now. There was just enough time left to watch the children in the nativity play at school on Tuesday evening, the night they broke up for the holiday. Why little Peter

MASS OBSERVATION

In the days leading up to the Second World War, many northern towns were still part of the 'dark, satanic mill' environment that William Blake described in 'Jerusalem'. The skyline was dotted with smoking factory chimneys and the housing of the working classes was epitomised by row upon row of terraces. The hooter summoning workers from their homes to start the morning shift had the cobbled streets ringing to the sound of clogs that sparked as they clipped the stones underfoot in scenes that would inspire Salford's LS Lowry to paint some of his most memorable representations of life in those days. One of his most famous works, the 1953 'Going to the Match', later purchased by the Professional Footballer's' Association, showed Lancashire folk enjoying one of their few moments of relief from working drudgery as they flocked to Burnden Park ready to cheer on the Wanderers in a Division One game. It was also true that 'a man may work from sun to sun, but a woman's work was never done', as a song from as far back as the 17th century so aptly put it. Monday morning was the traditional day when the week's laundry had to be seen to and row upon row of washing

was hung out on the line to dry in the sooty air. The shirts danced in the breeze like those in a Rael Brook TV advert that was popular in the 1960s.

The photographs in this section of our book date from the early years of the work of the social research organisation known as Mass Observation, which began formally in 1937. In the years leading up to then many social commentators and largely left wing thinkers expressed the wish to examine the daily lives of ordinary Britons and the environment in which they lived. However, it took the combined efforts of a trio of young men, part of a larger group of like minded friends, to put these interests into practice in a structured manner. Their background was about as far removed from working class Britain as one could imagine, but even they were aware of the sort of conditions in which ordinary families existed. Taking a bath in the front room by the only fire in the house was the norm for both young and old, though the tin bath brought in from the back yard for the adults was considerably larger than that used to perform the baby's ablutions that we see here!

Tom Harrisson (1911-76) was a Harrow educated anthropologist who had studied the life of natives in the New Hebrides. Charles Madge (1912-96) had a similarly privileged education, having attended Winchester College, and was well regarded as a poet and sociologist. They were complemented by a member of the Blackheath group of artists, Humphrey Jennings (1907-50), another university graduate. His special talent in photography would be of immense value to the Mass Observation programme. In early 1937, Madge and Jennings wrote to the New Statesman, outlining their ideas for a project to encourage a national panel of volunteers to reply to regular questionnaires on a variety of matters. Harrisson was interested in conducting an anthropological study in Britain, having concluded that it was all very well to observe life overseas, but there was apparently little recorded about our own way of life within these shores. He

contacted the other two and they decided to combine their studies under one umbrella and so the Mass Observation project came to fruition. Britain was still in the throes of the Depression, those dreadful interwar years when the ranks of the unemployed topped 3 million at one stage.

Men with nothing to do hung around street corners. Leaning against the traffic lights, near to the turning into Bank Street, the body language of the men suggests a sense of despair that the project wished to portray as an accurate representation of the situation in which so many Britons found themselves at the time. House ownership was out of the question, as many had trouble paying the rent to private landlords or the council. The building of new estates, such as Leverhulme Park, meant little to those who had just the pittance of dole money with which to feed and clothe their families.

The estate was named for William Hesketh Lever (1851-1925), the local soap magnate who founded Port Sunlight and developed the company that was to become the Unilever empire. On his elevation to the peerage in 1917, he combined his surname with his wife's maiden name to become Lord Leverhulme. To those of us now living in houses that might be worth an amount where three zeroes are tacked onto the £395 price of a semi detached in 1937, the cost of bricks and mortar seems ridiculously cheap. However, in real terms, this amount was far out of the reach of people for whom a white fiver meant untold riches.

The Mass Observation survey was conducted by two main bodies. There was a team of paid investigators who recorded people's conversations and made detailed notes about their behaviour. These were taken in a variety of situations, at work, at leisure, in meetings or simply out and about on the streets.

Even housewives taking a dubious look at a quack medicine stall in the open market were included in the photographer's list of behaviours to be recorded. Not everyone took kindly to such intrusion and a number of subjects objected forcibly to being spied upon and having 'nosey parkers', as they referred to them, poking into their business. It followed that part of the study was conducted in a clandestine manner, with shots being taken through hidden or disguised lenses. During the

Bolton. Although initially fascinated with his work, the intrusion into people's lives caused him to become stressed to such a degree that, after the war, he abandoned photography and took up painting and textile design instead. The in the field researchers sent their observations and findings to a second body, the National Panel. This was composed of people drawn from all over the country who kept diaries or regularly contributed to questionnaires sent to them by the central team.

war Duff Cooper was the Minister for Information and the information gatherers were sometimes referred to as 'Cooper's Snoopers'. Humphrey Spender (1910-2005) was one of the main photographers employed in the survey in

Quite what those in the ivory towers of the south of England made of this pair of little lads performing their own tableau of Le Manneken Pis in Brussels was not recorded in any great detail! No doubt verbal comments about school records and the like were made at the time. Spender took about 900 photographs in the late 1930s at Harrisson's request. Bolton had been selected as 'Worktown', an archetypical place where life in a northern industrial town could be observed. Harrisson had already spent some time working in a local mill as part of his own research so, when the Mass Observation project was established, it seemed sensible to him to focus on a place that he already knew to some extent. It was a time when young intellectuals were embracing left wing ideals and were looking to counter the social inequalities that they felt existed in Britain. Harrisson and his colleagues decided to observe them and bring them to the country's attention via published works. Some left wingers went off to fight fascism in the Spanish Civil War, while another group that included Burgess, Maclean, Philby and Blunt actively worked for the communists and sold their country out to the Soviets.

There was no suggestion that the members of the Mass Observation survey were motivated by anything other than fine principles, but it was necessary for them to record times of unrest to present an accurate picture of British society generally and, in these instances, of Bolton's way of life in particular. The meeting in Queen's Park during the apprentices' strike reflected the frustration felt by so many at the time. The dole queues were lengthy and the anxiety felt by ordinary folk had led to the famous Jarrow Crusade in late 1936 when over 200 unemployed Geordies set off to march on London in an effort to lobby Parliament and advertise their plight. In those days unemployment benefit ran out after 26 weeks, leaving men totally bereft of financial means.

Poverty went hand in hand with sickness and disease. This was a decade before the National Health Service was founded and doctors' bills were too much for ordinary folk. Many turned to quacks and self styled 'professors' of medicine who operated on street corners, travelling wagons or out of market stalls. This practitioner, looking like a cross between Ken Dodd and Max Wall, set himself up as a hair specialist. His potions for alopecia, dandruff and ringworm would have been largely ineffective as it was diet and housing conditions that were at the root cause of most people's problems.

For much of the 1930s, the country was ruled by the

National Government. In 1929 J Ramsay MacDonald became Prime Minister, leading a minority Labour government that limped along until 1931 when a National Government, involving representatives from the three major parties, was formed. This 'all in one' party won the general election in a landslide. MacDonald continued as leader until succeeded by Stanley Baldwin and, subsequently, Neville Chamberlain. During the war, it became known as the Coalition Government, with Winston Churchill at the helm for the most part, and no individual party held complete control until late 1945 when Clement Attlee's Labour Party swept to power. Children were often used as vehicles to promote a particular political party at both national and local level. On this occasion, in the 1937 local elections, coloured paper hats were distributed so that kiddies could show off their parents' allegiances, even if those wearing the colours had little idea of what it was that they were promoting.

Those who did have some money to spare in 1938 could spend it on two of the most popular forms of entertainment around. Every other Saturday, the Trotters were at home, playing top class opposition. The Bolton Wanderers' Burnden Park ground was one of the biggest and best in the country. It was often used to host semi final FA Cup games, as well as the usual league matches. Huddersfield Town was the opposition at the end of January and that would have been a top class match. The Yorkshire outfit was a powerhouse in the 1920s, winning three successive Division One titles, and was still a major attraction when it crossed the Pennines to fulfil this fixture. Cinema-going was at its height in the late 1930s, even during this period of recession. Early in the week, patrons could enjoy seeing the tall, blonde, 25-year-old Jean Muir star in the exciting movie, 'Cave-In'. Released in America as 'Draegerman Courage', it told the story surrounding heroism during a Nova Scotia gold mining disaster. By the weekend, top box office star Olivia de Havilland headed the billing for 'Call it a Day', a fairly mediocre comedy about a day in the life of an upper crust British family. The posters on the billboard were not limited to advertising leisure activities. They also included notices relating to local and national politics. One poster was devoted to a meeting being held in support of George Tomlinson, prospective Parliamentary candidate at the forthcoming Farnworth by-election. Ellis Smith, a Stoke-on-Trent MP, was to speak on his behalf. Tomlinson was successful and served Farnworth until 1952, rising to become the Minister for Education during Attlee's postwar Labour government.

The tannoy on top of the car or van was another popular tool of the political advertising trade. This one, used by the Labour Party, had attracted a group of interested children, though they were more interested in technology than political doctrine. Microphones, loudspeakers and shiny motors were more gripping than glib phrases about change, peace and future prosperity. Kiddies used to rush out into the street when the loudspeaker van came around. The more precocious would yell rude things at the party worker trying to pass on some political wisdom through the speakers. Actually, most of it was a waste of time, as most adults seldom changed their political colours from one year to the next. The Mass Observation programme in 'Worktown', or Bolton as it really was, reached its heights during the period from 1937 to 1940, but other research continued for another 30 years.

These children leaving Sunday School will be approaching 80 by now. Is the world a better place than the one in which they grew up? Each individual can decide the answer to that conundrum, though we can safely make the observation from the evidence of this final photograph that it must have felt safer on the streets, as these little ones are off on their way home without the need for an adult escort. Tom Harrisson returned to the Far East after the war and Charles Madge lectured in sociology at Birmingham University for 20 years. Humphrey Jennings became a film director, but was killed in a climbing accident in Greece, aged just 43. The Mass Observation archive is held at the University of Sussex. If it holds the truth about everyday people, as its pioneers hoped, then its creation was worthwhile.

THE WAR YEARS

Below: They hung out the bunting at Deane in November 1918 as the first world war came to an end. As well as the Union flags, an effigy of Kaiser Bill was strung up high. The children posing for the camera were told that this had been the war to end all wars, but they would come to know the lie of such sentiments when the balloon went up again just over 20 years later. These little tots knew all about hard times. Their fathers, uncles and elder brothers had been absent for up to four years, serving King and country in some of the most atrocious conditions ever experienced on battlefields. Many never returned, leaving widows and orphans to try to struggle on without the breadwinners in society. The government told them that homes fit for heroes would be created, but that turned out to be yet another hollow promise. So many of these youngsters grew into adulthood facing rising unemployment and poverty as the depression years took hold. Yet, it had all seemed so different back in the late summer of 1914. A patriotic fervour swept the nation as men proudly marched off to war, telling everyone that it would be all over by Christmas, Sadly, for many that was chillingly true as they perished on the banks of the Marne or the trenches at Ypres.

Right: We know that boy soldiers have been used by different armies over the years, but this was taking things a little too far. Roy Booth received his call up papers to enlist in the army at the height of World War Two. That he was only nine years of age caused him to become a minor celebrity for a short while. The idea of a short trousered junior school pupil heading off to take on the might of the Third Reich caused some merriment at the time. Even so, there were instances in World War One when boys, admittedly not as young as Roy, lied about their age in order to serve their country. Some were just into teenage when they tried to enlist and a few managed to do so, aided by recruiting sergeants who were paid a bonus on the numbers who signed up. Of course, the example here was all an administrative error and little Roy was able to enjoy his brief time in the spotlight before returning to the daily puzzle of long multiplication and learning his spellings. Happily for him, the enemy surrendered long before he was needed to join his peers on some foreign field.

Left: In the late 1930s, as the outbreak of war seemed a certainty, civil defence groups began organising their strategies and trained members in the use of measures that would help combat the effects of modern warfare on the civilian population. The issuing of gas masks and instruction in their use was one such measure. Newsreel footage from the Spanish Civil War emphasised that hostilities would include the bombing of industrial centres and cities and could possibly involve the use of gas and other noxious chemicals. All schoolchildren were issued with them in the early summer of 1939 and they carried them in purpose built boxes to and from lessons. At the start of September 1939, any youngster being evacuated from the major urban areas clutched a battered suitcase in one hand and a gas mask in the other. Babies also had special helmets into which mothers would have to pump air with a bellows. Even the police were expected to don the less than flattering apparatus, but it was a wise precaution even if the fear of a gas attack never materialised.

Below: Operation Pied Piper saw thousand upon thousand of children packed into railway carriages and buses in the first few days of the last war. They were packed off as evacuees to safer parts of the country in an attempt to protect them from the air raids that the country knew would come. Many returned home within a few months as we entered the period we now call 'the phoney war'. The children were homesick and their parents missed them as well, so the majority took their chances together. However, there were others who were evacuated because the threat of the enemy was right there on their doorstep and these youngsters would not be going home for a very long time. In 1940, some 300 British troops were stationed in the Channel Isles, but they were withdrawn as news of an impending invasion reached the government's ears and so left the islanders to their own devices. Not surprisingly, there was a large degree of bitterness directed towards London. With no clear direction from the British government, it was left up to the families to decide whether they wanted their children to leave for the mainland or not. The Germans invaded in June and stayed for nearly five years. Pictured here are some of those who made it to Bolton. Natalie Houguez, later Mrs N Jeanne, is the girl in the centre wearing the address label on her coat. Her siblings, Reginald and Barbara, are standing beside her, and her teenage aunts, Betty, Joan and Iris are also in the photograph.

Below: It was that feeling of helplessness that got to you. When the bombs fell, all that you could do was take shelter and then hope and pray that your house was one of the lucky ones. If this were true, then it meant that someone else had suffered and, though we could not rejoice at another's misfortune, then at least we could breathe a sigh of relief on our own behalf. But, where the hail of destruction did hit, people were initially numbed. Bodies were taken off to the mortuary and the injured patched up at the hospital. Those who survived unscathed looked literally shell shocked at the scale of the damage. This was not just their houses, but their homes that the Luftwaffe had destroyed. In October 1941, Punch Street, off Deane Road, was wrecked. The death toll here and nearby stood at 11. These were people who grew up together and each family felt another's pain. In the aftermath workmen started to clear the rubble, always conscious of finding some gruesome remains underneath the debris. Bowler hatted council officials discussed what to do, but there was little they could do for those who had lost precious mementoes of normality, such as a favourite teddy bear or the wedding album full of treasured photographs. Anyway, life would never again be the same, whatever the men in suits decided.

Right: During the last war there were frequent salvage drives. It was a waste not, want not culture and full of suggestions about making do and mending. Raw materials were scarce and anything that could be recycled was put to use. Those of us in the 21st century who think of ourselves as being 'green', and of being among the first to counteract the throwaway society, should look back to the 1940s. Here, children at Eagley collected all sorts of stuff that could be turned into something useful. Anything from an old envelope to a garden rail was collected and transported to a sorting centre. There, armies of volunteers sifted and graded rags, bones, paper, metal and any other items that could be put to further use. Throughout the war years appeals for junk and salvage were ongoing. Sometimes we were asked to hand over old saucepans, flat irons and bedsteads to provide scrap metal for the building of new warships and planes. It seemed ironic that the Spitfire overhead might really be a flying frying pan. Not to worry, as long as it did its job. The British, weaned on a diet of jumble sales and white elephant stalls, were past masters (and mistresses) at scavenging. The skill was to serve them well.

Below: As the outbreak of war became inevitable, many men joined up in advance and became part of the Territorial Army or other National Service organisations. The football season began as normal in the late summer of 1939, but only three Football League matches were played before activities were suspended for the duration of the war. The government issued a ban on mass assemblies. Though this was later relaxed as it saw the value of morale boosting sporting occasions, organised professional sport as we knew it ceased until the end of the war. Two professional football clubs saw their playing staff enlist virtually en masse. West Ham United and Bolton Wanderers' players swapped their playing kits for uniforms and prepared to face the foe.

Bolton's servicemen included Jack Ithell, Danny Winter, Jack Roberts, George Catterall, Don Howe and Harry Goslin, seen here striding out proudly as members of the 53rd field regiment RA (Bolton Artillery). In total, 32 of the 35 Wanderers' playing staff joined up, with the remainder working down the mines or in munitions. Harry Goslin, as the club captain, was the prime mover behind the mass enlistment. Sadly, he became one of those lost on a foreign field. He had survived the evacuation from the beaches at Dunkirk, but fell during the Mediterranean campaign on 18 December, 1943, in Italy. Goslin had risen through the ranks to achieve the status of lieutenant and was an example to others of duty before self.

The role of women in two world wars cannot be underestimated. In earlier times, men went off to do battle with Napoleon's troops, to the Crimea, to Afghanistan or South Africa in their many thousands, but the 20th century conflicts were something else. They departed in their millions, leaving behind factories, engineering works, farms and public transport vehicles without anyone to operate them. Step forward the fair sex. They tilled the fields and chopped down trees. Women handled heavy engineering plant and served in factories geared up for the war effort. They got behind the wheel of ambulances, tractors and trams and even took on new skills, such as servicing aeroplanes for the Royal Flying Corps. Towards the end of the war, those with a particular determination put on uniforms and joined the Women's Auxiliary Army Corps or Women's Royal Air Force.

It was more of the same, but on a larger scale and with greater organisation, the second time round. When the balloon went up in 1939, there were already women's organisations officially in place. Stella, Lady Reading, founded her Women's Voluntary Service in 1938 and her members had already played their part in preparing the public for war on the home front with various civil defence training exercises. As men set off overseas, yet again women juggled home and family management with the demands of keeping the wheels of industry and food production turning. The Land Army was reformed in July 1939. Some 113,000 women, a third of all those employed in agricultural work, had done their bit in the service that was introduced in 1917. When peace was declared in 1945, there were 460,000 women in uniform and 6.5 million in civilian war work.

Above: 'What are you doing, mister?' This warden was using the telephone box as a handy resting spot as he filled out some return or checked a particular detail on his log of events. He was a member of the Air Raid Precautions (ARP) team of civilians who offered their services as volunteers on the home front. Many were in jobs that had a protected status as their work expertise was invaluable to wartime production. Others were too old or unfit to join up, but still wanted to play their part. There was also a small handful who just enjoyed being officious and belonged to what came to be known as the 'jobsworth' mentality. Such a type was admirably portrayed by Bill Pertwee as Warden Hodges in the BBC sitcom 'Dad's Army'. During the blackout cries of 'Put that light out' and 'Don't you know there's a war on?' were often mimicked by comedians as part of their variety acts, but most wardens played an important role during the grim days of the early 1940s when we were under attack. They were often in the thick of it, assisting the general public find shelter during an air raid. They also reported the extent of bomb damage and assessed the local need for help from the emergency and rescue services. The wardens used their knowledge of their local areas to help find and reunite family members who had been separated during an air raid.

Below: During World War II all sorts of essential and non-essential foods were rationed, as well as clothing, furniture and petrol. Before the Second World War started Britain imported about 55 million tons of food a year from other countries. After war was declared in September, 1939, the British government had to cut down on the amount of food it brought in from abroad and decided to introduce a system of rationing. People were encouraged to provide their own food at home. The 'Dig for Victory' campaign started in October, 1939, and called for every man and woman to keep an allotment. Lawns and flowerbeds were turned into vegetable gardens. Chickens, rabbits, goats and pigs were reared in town parks and gardens. Ration Books were issued to make sure everybody got a fair share. They contained coupons that had to be handed to the shop keepers every time rationed goods were bought. Food was was the first to be rationed. On 8 January 1940, bacon, butter and sugar were rationed. Clothing rationing began on June 1st, 1941. There was a shortage of materials to make clothes. People were also urged to 'Make do and mend' so that clothing factories and workers could be used to make items, such as parachutes and uniforms, needed in the battle against Germany. Every item of clothing was given a value in coupons. Each person was given 66 coupons to last them a year. Later it was reduced to 48 coupons. Children were allocated an extra 10 clothing coupons above the standard ration to allow for growing out of clothes during a year. This did not prevent children having to wear 'hand me downs' from older brothers and sisters. In a make do and mend environment, trousers and skirts were patched and darned, old jumpers were unpicked and the wool used to make new garments. Rationing continued even after the war ended. Fourteen years of austerity in Britain ended at midnight on 4 July, 1954, when restrictions on the sale and purchase of meat and bacon were lifted.

AT LEISURE

No, this is not an LS Lowry print, though it has a look of one. It is a real photograph, taken in abput 1950 at Doffcocker Lodge. Obviously, it was snapped during one of the very cold winter spells that were much more common then than they are today. Skaters and cyclists, not to mention the occasional dog, enjoyed venturing out onto the frozen waters of the reservoir that had been created in 1874 when Doffcocker Brook was dammed to create a mill lodge. Flanked by Chorley Old Road on one side and Heaton Avenue and Moss Bank Way on two others, it was a popular place for people to visit. Always a great spot for anglers, it was designated an official nature reserve in 1992. It supports a large and varied range of plants. These make up a number of different habitat types that include marshes and swamps, grasslands and areas of scrub woodland. It is also notable for its bird life, in particular waders and wildfowl. Birds of prey, such as sparrowhawk, kestrel, tawny owl, hobby and peregrine have also been recorded. The site hosts populations of water vole, pipistrelle bat, shrew and weasel. However, skaters have to go further afield now in search of somewhere to practise their pastime. Even those on roller skates have missed out since the Navada burned down in 1985.

the local bakery giant. In more recent times it has become known as the Hoover Bolton Band. Brass bands have traditionally been associated with industry. Everywhere from textile factories to the coalmines seemed to have their own special unit. Communities were fiercely proud of the musicianship displayed by the men and women who represented them. The ruling classes patronisingly called it 'cloth cap music'. However, the effect of the bands on the working classes was enormous and provided one of the first mediums for both musical and social opportunities to the masses. They flourished in the Victorian age and gradually found people willing to contribute original music just for their genre. In more modern times, brass band music has hit the pop charts, as when Brighouse and Rastrick performed 'The Floral Dance', and also been the main storyline in a movie, 'Brassed Off' starring Pete Postlethwaite.

Below: Rivington Hall Barn is a listed building with a genuine Anglo Saxon design. It measures 105 feet by 57 feet and stands 23 high. The interior features original wooden beams. The earliest records of the manor were written in 1202. The Great House Barn, outside which the cars in this early 1950s photograph were parked, is a tea room and gift shop. The design is Scandinavian and the barn was subject to major renovation in 1702. The roof is spectacular with an internal oak framework. During the last war, it was used by units of the Territorial Army. Rivington village and the surrounding countryside that includes Lever Park has attracted generations of locals to come and picnic or indulge

Above: This was the official programme for the speedway meeting held on 6 April 1929. Raikes Park was home to the dirt and cinder track spectacle that thrilled the crowds, but it was a short lived venture. The 440 yard circuit had its first meeting on 20 August, 1928, though it had been used for greyhound racing in the previous year. Speedway was promoted by local motor cycle dealers MF Edwards and A Horrocks. Under the banner of The Lancashire Dirt Track Racing Association, the inaugural event attracted 6,000 spectators as Norman Dawson rode to victory in the Senior Cup. The local rider 'Tiger Jack' Wood, the 'Bolton Broadsider', cut his teeth on this circuit before heading for Europe where he built himself a formidable reputation. This programme turned out to be the penultimate one issued at the track as Bolton staged its one and only Dirt Track League match here a fortnight later against Preston. Despite winning 36-24, the club resigned from the league and Raikes Park went back to dog racing and, later, occasional stock car racing. The track closed in 1996.

Top right: Bolton Borough Prize Band, as it was known when photographed in the 1920s, has undergone various name changes over the years. At one time it was known as Bolton St Luke's and then Bolton Subscription Band. In the years to follow this picture, the 'Prize' part of the name was dropped. From 1985 until 1992, the band was run with assistance from Warburton's,

in an afternoon's stroll. It is unusual to see a motorcycle sidecar nowadays, but it was once a common sight as it afforded a small family with a cheap form of motoring as private car ownership was still too expensive for most ordinary folk. Seeing one always reminds older motorists of the days when AA and RAC riders used them and saluted members, identified by badges on their radiator grilles, as they drove past.

Above: They were off in their 'charras' for a day out. It might have been a trip into the countryside, but more likely it was for a visit to Blackpool to enjoy the sands, the prom, the kiss me quick hats, a show on the pier and a tour of the illuminations. That was what you called a full day trip. The men could have their jolly boys' outings, but the girls were just as able to have their own brand of fun. The female staff from the weaving sheds at Taylor and Hartley's Mill, in Bolton Road, Westhoughton enjoyed the opportunity to let their hair down and do so away from their husbands and sweethearts. At the seaside they could stroll arm in arm with one another and giggle to their hearts' content without anyone they knew frowning at them. On the way back, a stop off for some fish and chips was a must. They sang the hit songs of the day with great gusto and, as the coaches headed back up the last stretch of the road, they organised a whip round for the driver and thanked him with a rousing chorus of 'For he's a jolly good fellow'. Then, it was back home and up the wooden hill to bed, because that blessed hooter would soon be going to summon the workforce back to the mill.

Below: Now, there's posh. This photograph was taken on 23 December, 1949 in Smithills. Goodness, most people could not afford a radiogram, never mind a television back then. It would not be long, though, before this luxury became an essential part of family entertainment. Until then, an invitation to watch a programme on someone's private set was a privilege. It was the 1953 Coronation and that year's FA Cup Final that helped promote the invasion of the goggle box into all our lives. When those events occurred, people with TVs suddenly discovered that they were the most popular neighbours in the street as locals with whom they had seldom shared a conversation were able to negotiate an invite into the front room. After enjoying the entertainment offered by the splendour of the wedding coach on its way to Westminster Abbey and a seven goal thriller at Wembley, dads were instructed to put television high on the list of goods that they could get on hire purchase. To modern youth the tiny screens and fuzzy pictures would seem hilarious. But, to those of us who were around at the time, it was a magical experience. The kids had Muffin the Mule, Andy Pandy and The Flowerpot Men. Adults watched panel games like 'What's My Line' and exciting drama such as 'The Quatermass Experiment' until the little white dot on the screen faded.

Left: Moss Bank Park was opened to the public in 1922. It has been enjoyed by successive generations ever since and today youngsters love to ride on the model railway and see the peacocks roaming across the lawns. They also delight in the butterflies, birds and other creatures that are part of Animal World. The tower in the aviary was originally built as an astronomical observatory by John Horrocks Ainsworth, whose family used to live here. It was the start of the Easter weekend in April 1958 when this photograph was taken and, despite there being a distinct nip in the air, the park was crowded with people enjoying the holiday period. The baby in the pram owed those rosy cheeks as much to the biting wind as to a healthy constitution. The boy, properly dressed of course in his school cap, was aboard a tricycle that has become something of a collector's item. The Gresham Flyer had a little boot at the back where the lad could store anything from a puncture repair kit to his latest copy of the Beano. It also had a telescopic handle so that dad could regulate junior's rate of acceleration and keep him close to hand. The boy does not look too thrilled. He would have been happier pretending to be Reg Harris and go racing ahead.

Top: Going to a league match at Burnden Park was a fortnightly ritual for many of us during the soccer season. There were different ways of getting there, but the bicycle was a most popular method for those who did not have a car or wanted to save on bus fare. The streets around the ground were full of bikes that were left in back alleys and yards. For some house occupiers there was a small business opportunity here. At 2 pm every other Saturday someone would be on duty up to kick-off time, collecting cash from cyclists for the privilege of parking their bikes in a safe environment. For a modest sum, equivalent to about a penny in current money, the rider could leave his favoured mode of transport in good hands. It was a small price to pay, secure in the knowledge that, a couple of minutes after the ref blew the final whistle, the fan could reclaim his bike and pedal home. If he lived close enough, he might just make it back in time for the opening strains of the 'Sports Report' signature tune on the radio as he settled down to listen to the football results from around the country. As the stirring sound of 'Out of the Blue' faded and Eamonn Andrews started speaking, an hour of soccer on the wireless awaited.

Below: Manxmen did not know what had hit them when this bevy of Bolton beach belles arrived on the island in the early 1960s. Topless bathing was for the naughty French sands and definitely not to be considered at Douglas or Port Erin. Continental holidays, in any case, were still out of reach for most of the working classes, but the tide would soon turn. Package trips to Spain and camping holidays in Brittany would prove both attractive and affordable. In the meantime, Anglesey and the Isle of Man were abroad, were they not? You had to cross water to get there, in any case. The journey that these young women made was via the ferry across the Irish Sea. They probably went from Heysham on a journey that lasted several hours, hoping that the water would not be too choppy or they would land at their destination looking a little green about the gills. Douglas was the main resort, with its many hotels and host of boarding houses that were run by matronly women who ruled with a rod of iron. Woe betide you if you were five minutes late for the evening meal. Six-thirty sharp meant just that. After a solid meal of soup, roast beef and spuds, followed by jam roly-poly, it was time to enjoy a horse drawn tram ride along the front.

Right: Modern circuses are little more than vehicles for acrobats, trapeze artists and contortionists. The old days when performing seals balanced beach balls on their noses, dogs jumped through blazing hoops and lions snarled at the tamer cracking the whip have long gone. We know that some animals were mistreated and that can never be condoned, but many others had a happy existence and enjoyed performing in the big tops. It was always a great occasion when the circus came to town. Forthcoming shows were advertised by a procession through the streets. Men on stilts towered above the crowds, handing out leaflets. Pretty girls in short, sequinned costumes cartwheeled along the road, gaily dressed clowns pretended to hurl buckets of water over squealing children, strong men flexed their muscles, riders got their horses to prance on two legs and, perhaps best of all, the elephants lumbered along, trunk to tail. However, this was a sight that was in decline even in May 1964. One newspaper report grumbled that a mere 15 elephants and 10 good looking girls was not the sort of parade that people expected when Billy Smart's Circus hit town. Chipperfield, Bertram Mills and Gerry Cottle are just some of the other names that conjure up fond memories.

Above: Ballroom dancing was still one of the most popular ways to spend a Saturday night in March 1957. How else could you get a handsome man in your arms without having to appear cheap? Although couples regularly went together to the Palais de Danse on Bridge Street, it was quite permissible for pairs of young women and unattached men to attend. The girls would sit shyly at their table on the edge of the dance floor, waiting for some potential beau to pluck up courage and come over and request the pleasure of a dance. Sometimes, you had to make an excuse if the lad in question was particularly spotty, but, more often than not, it was a case of granting him one dance and leaving it at that. Then, no-one's feelings were hurt. Usually, young men approached a pair of girls in matching twos. Why was it that your friend seemed to attract the one who was better looking? At least everyone could dance. It was a necessary requisite to be able to waltz, quickstep, foxtrot and cha-cha, so Chorlton's Dance Academy and the like did good business. There was always a live band playing at the Palais that threw in a few modern tunes to go with the older ones from the heydays of the big band sound. However, within a couple of years, the requests would include the playing of numbers that had been heard on 78 rpm records by singers with strange names like Elvis, Gene, Buddy and the like. Television's 'Come Dancing', introduced by George Elrick, was broadcast here on one occasion in 1958.

This group from Bolton were obviously enjoying themselves at Middleton Tower in June 1967. The golden age of the holiday camp was in the 50s and 60s. After the war there was a great rush to the coast. Many people had not had a holiday for years and could not wait to get away. The holiday camp provided what they were looking for. Prices were reasonable, food was plentiful and there was plenty to do, even when it was raining. The holiday camp sector expanded rapidly from the early ones built by Harry Warner and Billy Butlin in the 1930s. Many camps used by the forces in the war quickly became holiday camps. Quite a few had, in fact, been taken over for military use and once again opened their doors to holiday makers. In some cases, the campers moved in almost as the soldiers marched out. Middleton Tower, near Morecambe, opened in 1939, but was revamped in 1949 to include the SS Berengaria as its main building. This was created using relics from the Cunard cruise ship that had been scrapped a decade earlier. Consisting of 900 chalets, the camp was bought by Fred Pontin in 1964, making it the largest such establishment in his empire. As the attractions of holidays abroad outweighed those at home, the days of the large holiday camps were numbered. Middleton Tower closed in 1993.

Below: 'The Longest Day' was one of the most popular movies of the 1960s. With an all star cast, it depicted the action on the Normandy beaches on D-Day in June 1944. It was nominated for the best picture category at the Oscars and won an award for its photography. Despite being overly long, running for nearly three hours, it has been shown on television on many occasions. The movie was made in 1962, though the date on this photograph is October 1969. The Odeon cinema was part of the empire founded by Oscar Deutsch in the Midlands when he opened his picture house in Dudley in 1928. Most of the cinemas he had built conformed to a similar art deco style. Within a decade, such was the popularity of the new genre of 'talkie' films, there were 250 Odeons across Britain, with the flagship being the one on London's Leicester Square. Bolton's link in the chain began on 21 August, 1937. The First Battalion of the Royal Scots played a fanfare that was well received by an opening night audience of 2,000. The bill of fare was extensive, with a newsreel, cartoon and no fewer than three films to enjoy. The main feature, 'Dark Journey', starred two top box office names in Conrad Veidt and Vivien Leigh. It closed its doors in 1983, becoming a bingo hall.

Right: The good thing about a game of soccer is that you needed very little in the way of equipment when you were just a lad in the middle of the last century. We did not need designer shirts with Ronaldo or even Campo printed upon them. Nor was anyone worried that we might come to harm if we wandered off with a group of friends to the park or down the road a-ways. Who needed fancy nets or proper goalposts when we had coats to put down or a pair of sticks to shove into the ground? Pictured in the shadow of the gas works, the recreation ground or 'rec' at Spa Road, near Queen's Park, saw these boys using the only piece of equipment that was truly necessary, namely a ball. Sometimes a tennis ball sufficed, but it was best if you knew someone who had a 'casey'. He was a very popular lad, always being asked out to play, even if he was the most useless player imaginable. After lengthy use, the football would become worn and be about to split in places and the lacing sharp when you headed it, but who cared? We ran around in the fresh air, storming into tackles like Tommy Banks or indulging in Dougie Holden style dribbles.

Left: Snooker took off as a popular television sport with the advent of colour television in 1967 and probably peaked in the 1980s and early 1990s. However, some early commentators were a little slow to realise how their remarks came over to the watching public. 'For those watching in black and white, the blue ball is behind the green', had viewers in stitches. Originally, the game was thought to be just for the lower classes in society and was always linked with gambling and unsavoury elements. Yet, the major players developed a dress code and level of sportsmanship at the table that would have been the envy of the most refined of amateur, sporting gentlemen. Exhibition matches were very popular and professional players augmented the humble prize money available in competitions by spending time at holiday camps, billiard halls and private clubs. On this occasion, John Spencer and Alex Higgins posed for a picture before their challenge match at the Bolton Institute of Technology. Radcliffe born Spencer, a true gentleman of the baize cloth, had just become the world champion, a title he would win again in 1971 before becoming the first player to win at the new venue of The Crucible in Sheffield, where he lifted his third title. He was later to suffer from an eye disease that ended his career. He died in 2006. Higgins was a very popular, but temperamental, player. Aged just 20 in this photograph, he won the world title in 1972 and 1982.

Above: The Nab Gate pub and restaurant, near where this bevy of beauties stood in August 1972, was then a relatively new building, having replaced one pulled down in the late 1950s. An inn had been on the site for the best part of 400 years, commanding an elevated position at the top of Hardy Mill Road at the junction with Stitch-me-Lane and Arthur Lane, in Harwood. The pub's name was derived from nab, meaning 'hill', and the toll gate that once stood here on the old turnpike. The ladies, regulars at the Nab Gate, were about to enjoy a day's outing. They sported the very latest in early 70s fashion, with mini skirts still in vogue for some. The one with the leather boots had a hemline that our dads used call a pelmet when they were banging on about the appalling fashions of the modern era, as they used to complain. We took no notice, of course, and made our hair bigger as well, just to get them going.

Left: If they really are the best years of your life, then it is occasions like this that helped to make our time at school so memorable and happy. These lads from Smithills School were enjoying the freedom of a holiday at a camp in Grasmere, in the Lake District, in June 1967. Such field visits and adventure holidays were part and parcel of the academic year for many schools, along with Saturday morning soccer matches and after school clubs. These were only made possible by the dedication and time put in by teachers who knew that sitting in a classroom was only part of the educational process. These sorts of activities became more restricted in the final quarter of the last century.

In August 1973, youngsters had great fun in the summer sunshine as they splashed about in the paddling pool at Queen's Park. The park was created from land purchased from several sources. The Ecclesiastical Commission and two local people, simply known as Miss Pilkington and Mr Topping, sold the land to the Corporation in the mid 1860s. William Henderson, a Birkenhead designer, drew up the plans for the park that was opened on 24 May, 1866, by the Earl of Bradford.

Simply known as Bolton Park, it took on its current name in 1897 to honour Queen Victoria's Diamond Jubilee. Its peaceful trappings were disrupted by a Zeppelin raid on 26 September, 1916, but it has more generally echoed to the shouts of happy kiddies than the noise of exploding bombs. A natural history museum, built by Samuel Chadwick, opened here in 1884. It closed in 1955 and was demolished two years later, its contents having been transferred to Bolton Museum.

BOLTON
WANDERERS

Above: Bolton Wanderers belongs to the exclusive list of clubs who formed the inaugural Football League in 1888. Of the original 12 founder members only Accrington failed to survive. Founded in 1874 by Reverend John Farrall Wright as Christ Church FC, the club changed its name to Bolton Wanderers three years later and became a professional side in 1880. It played at Pike's Lane until 1895 when Burnden Park opened. These players were the ones who were the first to grace the turf that was to be home for over a century. The previous year, the Trotters made it to the FA Cup Final, played at Goodison Park, but went down to a strong Notts County side. A decade later, defeat again greeted the team when Manchester City won at Crystal Palace. The next cup final that Bolton reached was one of the most memorable ever staged. We met West Ham United in the first ever Wembley final. This was the one remembered by everyone for the huge crowds and the white police horse that tried to marshal them. With David Jack scoring the first goal at the new venue, Bolton went on to triumph 2-0.

Right: When this view of Burnden Park was photographed the 1966 World Cup was upon us. Sadly, for local supporters, this stadium was not selected to host any of the games. Whilst you could not argue about Old Trafford and Goodison Park being chosen, the choice of both Roker Park and Ayresome Park in the northeast lacked inspiration. Small crowds, even for a quarter final game, epitomised the Wearside and Teesside interest. It is not as if Bolton's ground was considered inappropriate. Burnden Park played host to many FA Cup semi finals over the years and did so in World Cup year. Everton beat Manchester United in front of a crowd that was three times the size of some of those who watched the international matches a few months later. Situated just a mile from the town centre, it had easy access on foot, by bus and rail. For those who came by car, a large parking area was available. The club had its home here from 1895 to 1997, before relocating to the Reebok, out near Horwich.

Right: They never had a chance, with the Fates lined up against them. Just as it would be again in 1958, when public sentiment supported Bolton's opponents, everyone outside the town prayed for Blackpool to win the 1953 FA Cup Final. Stanley Matthews, one of the most popular players of his generation, had won everything in the game except for a cupwinner's medal. Now 38, this would surely be the Blackpool winger's last opportunity when the two Lancashire sides met at Wembley. Although Stan Mortensen knocked in a hat-trick for the seasiders, the match was dubbed 'the Matthews' final' because of his contribution in the closing stages that culminated in his crossing the ball for Bill Perry to settle the game 4-3. In truth, Bolton's players were hard done by. Although Eric Bell scored to give the Wanderers a 3-1 lead midway through the second half, by then he was a virtual passenger, having sustained a nasty injury earlier on. No substitutes were allowed and a weakened Bolton could not hang on. When the boys returned home they were given a heroes' welcome nonetheless. The players waved to the fans, who numbered about 10,000, as they made their way through Farnworth. Holden and Lofthouse would return five years later as victors, but for the others the chance of glory never knocked at the door again.

Below: Football at its grass roots level needs all the support it can get. It was good to see Nat Lofthouse, an international centre forward, giving Bolton Wyresdale FC a good send off as it left for a tour of Denmark in the 1950s. Amateur sides and semi-professional outfits have always needed help from supporters, officials and wellwishers in the local community to survive. So often, professional superstars turn their noses up at those they class as beneath their station, but Nat was not one of that ilk. He was always happy to put himself out for a good cause and if his presence as the Wyresdale coaches rolled out of town could be of use, then he went home a contented man. He was Bolton born and bred and liked nothing better than doing his bit for his home town.

Above: Eddie Hopkinson was a relieved man when a shot from Bobby Charlton (out of picture) clipped the post during the 1958 FA Cup Final. However, it was one of the few occasions when he looked worried during the match as Manchester United were outplayed for most of the 90 minutes. Bolton, though, were not popular winners. It was not their fault, but the country had naturally swung behind the Busby Babes after the terrible Munich plane cash that February had decimated the side. Somehow, a patched up team of reserves and other clubs' cast-offs managed to win through to Wembley. Crash survivors Gregg and Foulkes played throughout the cup run. Charlton and Viollet were patched up both physically and mentally in order to help out, but it was too much to ask. Wanderers had a tough, no nonsense defence who, it was said, took no prisoners. Behind them, Hopkinson was an able custodian. Perhaps his lack of inches caused others to have doubts about him, but he played 14 games for England and 578 for Bolton, a club record.

Below left: Even the most blinkered Bolton Wanderers fan raised a quizzical eyebrow at the very least when, early in the second half of the 1958 FA Cup Final, Manchester United goalkeeper Harry Gregg seemed to be about to catch the ball near his own goal line when Nat Lofthouse thundered into him. The referee was about the only man in Wembley Stadium who thought that Bolton's centre forward had charged Gregg fairly. A stunned keeper joined the ball in the back of the net and we were on our way to a 2-0 victory, Lofthouse having already opened the scoring early in the game. Wags remarked that whenever Gregg saw Lofthouse in the street thereafter he always ducked. It was the second year running that there was a controversial incident concerning a United goalie. In the previous final against Aston Villa, Ray Wood was concussed and had his cheekbone broken by Peter McParland in another so-called fair shoulder charge. In neither case did the Manchester United players kick up a fuss. They may have had a few comments to make, but no one surrounded the referee and there was no mass maul as would happen today. Wood's injury ruined that game, but at least the 1958 one was not similarly spoiled. Nat Lofthouse was Bolton's skipper and inspiration. His talents were recognised by the England selectors and he made 33 appearances for his country in the 1950s. Dubbed the 'Lion of Vienna' after one memorable performance, Nat continued to serve his club in a variety of capacities after retiring from playing. He was awarded the OBE in 1997.

Above: Born in late 1948, Frank Worthington came from a Halifax footballing family and signed for Huddersfield Town in 1966. He left for Leicester in 1972 and stayed there for five years before moving to Bolton in 1977. He played 84 games for the Wanderers, netting 35 goals. Frank scored one of the most memorable goals seen on any soccer ground in 1979 in a match against Ipswich Town. With his back to goal, he juggled the ball on his knee and instep, flicked it up over his shoulder, performed a neat pirouette before stroking the ball into the net past a bemused keeper. Even the referee was moved to applaud him as he trotted back to the centre circle. But that was Frank. He was a flamboyant and exciting player, noted for his Elvis style sideburns and flowing mane. Frank made no secret of his enjoyment of the high life and this was probably part of the reason that such a wonderful player only collected eight England caps. Here Frank is seen stroking a penalty in his usual confident manner, watched by the first £1 million man, Trevor Francis of Nottingham Forest. He left Bolton in 1979 and played for a host of other clubs, retiring from English League football in 1988 having made 757 appearances and scoring 234 goals.

EVENTS & OCCASIONS

The coronation of George VI brought to a conclusion the most difficult time the monarchy had undergone for centuries. The antics of Edward VIII and the secrecy of the government had thrown what had seemed to be a stable institution, respected and revered across the Commonwealth, into disarray. The politicians slapped censorship notices on the press, preventing publication of gossip about the king's affair with the twice divorced Wallis Simpson, even though it was well publicised in America and the rest of Europe. When the news finally broke at home and the king abdicated the country was divided in its sympathies. But it came together in May 1937 as it joined with nations as far flung as Fiji and Canada, Tonga and the Gold Coast to celebrate the start of a period of royal equilibrium once more. The flags and standards flying the length of Centre Street, Brownlow Fold, displayed the depth and extent of the feeling expressed here and across the British Commonwealth of Nations, as it was called until 1946. The date chosen for the coronation was the very one originally set aside for Edward VIII. By then, he was in France preparing for his marriage to the woman who had cost him the crown. The royal family never accepted her into their midst, though the Duke of Windsor, as he was to become, was reconciled to some degree in later years.

Above: They made an incongruous couple as they strolled along Greenthorne, in Edgworth, in September 1931. She was the philanthropist Annie Barlow, an ardent supporter of many causes. Born in 1863, the youngest child of a textile magnate, Annie developed a strong interest in Egyptology following a visit to that country in 1887. She was involved in some of the excavations for ancient artefacts that fascinated fellow Victorians. Some of these are still held in Bolton Museum. Although lame from polio that she contracted as a child, she worked tirelessly right up to her death in 1941. Her unmistakable companion was none other than Mohandas Gandhi (1869-1948), more generally known as Mahatma. Born in the Indian state of Gujarat, he came to London in 1888 to study law. In the 1890s he was active in South Africa, railing against the oppression and racism direct at Indians living there and helping found civil rights movements in that country. He returned to India in 1915 and involved himself during the interwar years in the struggle for Indian independence. Non co-operation and peaceful resistance were the weapons that he used. It is ironic that he was murdered the year after India became independent from British rule.

Jim's sister Mary.

large publicity and soon there were similar demonstrations of physical exercise routines being performed across the country. Women in vests and shorts or leotards, swinging Indian clubs in time to the music, were seen long before the word aerobic was invented.

Below: Bernard Law Montgomery (1887-1976) was a distinctive figure in the traditional army beret that he usually wore. He attended The King's School, Canterbury, before graduating from Sandhurst and fought with distinction during World War I. He acquired a reputation as an efficient and tough leader. In 1940, after the evacuation at Dunkirk, Montgomery commanded the southeastern section of England in anticipation of a German invasion. In August 1942 he was appointed as the commander of the 8th Army in North Africa and helped restore the morale of troops on the run from Rommel's German forces. His stunning victory at El Alamein in November 1942 was one of the turning points of the war and the church bells in Britain were rung for the first time since hostilities began. Under the command of the American General Eisenhower, with whom he had a frosty relationship, Montgomery led the Allied invasion of Normandy on D-Day in 1944. He was made a viscount in 1946 and went on to become deputy commander of NATO in the 1950s. He became the 10th Freeman of Bolton in November 1949 and chatted with wellwishers before receiving the award. He also paid a visit to Bolton Lads' Club and Burnden Park. After his death in 1976 he was afforded a state funeral at St George's Chapel, Windsor.

Above: Westhoughton's British Legion Fete was held in the blazing sunshine of what was an excellent summer in 1937. As well as the events in the marquees, the exhibitions and the sideshows, the locals were treated to a display of fitness and agility by the 'Health and Grace Girls'. Keep fit was all the rage in the 1930s. There were no such things as gyms with walking machines, weight lifting suites, exercise bicycles and the rest. In fact, it was often open air activities that were promoted. Women were especially keen to demonstrate that they were not tied to the kitchen sink and wanted to show that they had athletic prowess. They learned to play tennis and soon were hitting forehands with stunning pace. No longer were they going to pat the ball feebly over the net. Golfing gear was donned and they strode across the course, mashie niblick in hand, ready to take on the most difficult of fairways. They swam like fishes and discarded the side saddle on their horses. In 1930, Mary (Mollie) Bagot Slack founded the Women's League of Health and Beauty in London and within three months had a membership of a thousand. An open air display in Hyde Park attracted

Left: Hough Lane throbbed with joyous activity and cheerful celebrations as the residents celebrated VE Day in May 1945. Victory in Europe had taken nearly six years to achieve and all that the children preparing to tuck in could remember of their young lives was being touched by shortages, fear and sadness. They were growing up surrounded by ration coupons, bomb craters and missing relatives. But those troubles were put to one side as they prepared to party. Every street in the country was like this one, bedecked with flags and bunting flying above trestle tables that had been borrowed from schools and church halls. Mums had pooled their meagre rations or blown a week's food coupons to put on the best spread the children had ever feasted upon. The buns might have been on the dry side as egg powder was not quite the same as the real thing, but they were buns after all. It was all far better than that revolting pie of swedes, turnips and parsnips that Lord Woolton recommended. We can be sure he never tasted it. After the celebratory tea someone found an old wind-up gramophone and put on a record of the hokey-cokey and everyone danced themselves silly. Whilst they cleared away the mothers sang quietly about bluebirds and Dover, shedding a small tear for those who never made it back for this or any other party.

Below: Residents on Drummond Street, just off the A666 Blackburn Road, were celebrating in fine style on 2 June 1953. It was Coronation Day and the nation went wild with joy as the Archbishop of Canterbury, Dr Fisher, placed the crown on the head of Queen Elizabeth II. The weather was not all it might have been, but who cared? It did not dampen our spirits, even if it made the fairy cakes and potted meat sandwiches go a little soggy at the street parties being held all over the land. The church hall had been raided for trestle tables and mums had slaved away over hot ovens to make the day that bit special. Fancy dress competitions were held and patriotic songs sung, rivalling the joyful scenes that were witnessed on VE Day at the end of the war. Union flags were hung from windowsills and jolly bunting draped from lampposts across the street as impromptu congas were danced on the pavement. The children thought the adults had gone mad, but that was not going to distract them from tucking into the goodies that lay on the tablecloths in front of them. The few who owned television sets suddenly found themselves very popular as neighbours crowded into their front rooms to watch the ceremonies being relayed from Westminster Abbey.

Election fever was raging on Kent Street, Farnworth, in 1950. Local residents made their allegiances clear with a variety of banners and posters proclaiming the benefits of having a Labour government. Of course, the industrial heartland of the north of England has long been the mainstay of the Labour Party, but these current and potential voters were taking no chances in getting their message across. If a van with a tannoy on top came round broadcasting a recommendation for the Tories, the children in the photograph chased after it booing and, occasionally, throwing rotten fruit at the intrepid right wing supporter on the microphone in the passenger seat. This was the year when the Labour government of Clement Attlee was to be tested in his first general election as its leader. He swept to power in 1945 in a landslide over Winston Churchill. The population wanted change after the war and, though the man with the 'V' sign and the big cigar was the one to win the war, Attlee was seen as the leader who could win the peace. However, despite instituting a policy of social reform, Labour failed to deliver the economic stability that people demanded. The February 1950 election saw Attlee squeak home with an overall majority of just five seats. The writing was on the wall and by the end of the following year another election saw Churchill regain the keys of 10 Downing Street.

Music, especially of the brass band variety, plays a significant part in the culture of northern England. Bolton is no exception in its appreciation of the uplifting sound of cornets, trombones and euphoniums blending together. Victoria Square has been the focal point for marches, parades and gatherings over the years, with the Town Hall acting as a magnificent centre piece. In these photographs we get an idea of the majesty of this fine building, with the strength of the mighty lion representing the important work taking place in the corridors of power behind him. Additionally, the concentration on the faces of the bandsmen tells us that they regard their music as a serious business. However, there is some light relief here as well. Just look at those two little imps leading the way in front of the drummers who are beating out a rhythmic tattoo as a marching beat and foundation for the instruments behind them. The youngsters are enjoying their moment in the spotlight and playing up to the camera for all they are worth. In the corresponding photograph, it would appear that Christmas is on the way. The tree to the right is illuminated and housewives with shopping bags have purchased a few items for the kiddies' stockings. On this occasion, carols would feature in the band's repertoire.

to be Britain's longest running soap opera. Playing the role of Stan Ogden, he filled the small screen almost literally with his large frame and considerable personality for another 20 years. His character was a beer swilling workshy individual, but something of a likeable rogue. Screen wife Hilda, brilliantly portrayed by Jean Alexander, with her flying ducks and penchant for 'muriels' on the wall, complemented him perfectly. Born Bernard Popley in 1914, 'Bunny', as he was nicknamed, had no theatrical family connections but spent his early life in repertory. After serving in the armed forces during the war, he returned to stage and film work. He joined Granada TV in 1956 as a continuity announcer, before eventually auditioning for the Stan Ogden role. His first immortal words on the show were, 'A pint of mild and 20

Above: Bernard Youens was not yet a household name when he was spotted at Bolton's Ideal Home Exhibition in 1964. He had just joined the cast of 'Coronation Street' in what would turn out

fags, missus'. A star was born. Youens suffered a series of heart attacks in the 1970s that left him with a slight speech defect and some mobility problems.

Below: Looking as pretty as a picture, May Queen, Jeanette Wood, led her attendants in the parade as she represented St Ethelbert's in 1970. Surely this photograph must hold a particularly special memory for her and pride of place in the childhood album. All the girls scrubbed up beautifully for this celebration and they loved every minute of the preparations as they preened and posed for ages, along with mums fussing over them in order that they looked their best. The page boys were a little more reticent. 'Give over mum' was a cry often heard as she smoothed down a wayward lock or straightened his collar for the 20th time. The girls holding the train were secretly envious of Jeanette's place at the head of the procession, but they tried not to let it show. Jeanette was a pupil at St Ethelbert's RC Primary School, on Melbourne Road, just off the A676 Wigan Road. The school celebrated its centenary in 2005.

Left: It was time for a good old knees up on Wilmot Street, Halliwell, in 1977. As part of the Queen's silver jubilee celebrations this group of neighbours decided to determine which of them had the knobbliest of joints. From the evidence on view it would appear to have been a dead heat involving several dozen. We had not had a proper national celebration since 1953, when Elizabeth II was crowned. But, despite the fears of some sceptics that support for the monarchy was on the wane, the whole country turned out in force during that warm, long summer. Street parties, reminiscent of VE Day, got together households who seldom acknowledged each other from one week to the next, a polite nod on the way to work. 'Liz rules OK' T-shirts sold out and jubilee mugs were sold in vast numbers. In 2002 there was the same worry that no one was all that interested in acknowledging the golden jubilee. What nonsense. The country poured out onto the streets and partied just as before.

Several knots of bystanders hung around the corners of the street around Folds Road on this gloomy day in 1941. They were witnessing the aftermath of a particularly nasty accident involving a pair of trams. Quite how they managed to collide with one another is difficult to understand, but they met with such force that the damage was extensive. Not only were the vehicles wrecked, but many passengers suffered major injuries. Thirty-one of those on board had to receive treatment for their wounds, the majority being on the tram that overturned. People had successfully dodged the bombs dropped by German aircraft in the blitz and were now laid low by machines manufactured in their own country. It was an unusual occurrence as this form of public transport was among the safest that was possible. In the history of Bolton's trams there were very few instances of nasty accidents. Those that did occur usually involved a careless pedestrian wandering in front of one of them or a car driver losing concentration and getting in the way. To have a pair of trams colliding was memorable in its rarity and very painful for a lot of those involved.

TRANSPORT

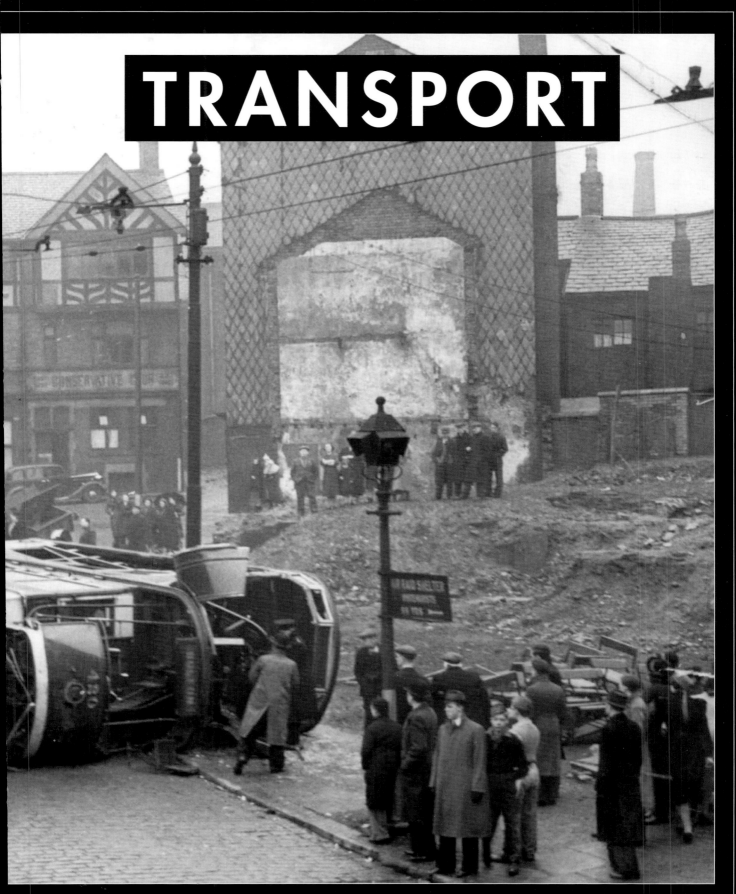

Right: This very early Bolton Corporation Tramways motor bus was a draughty affair for the driver. He needed a constitution of iron to work in our northern climate, notorious for its spells of driving rain and wind. Quite how he went on in the depths of winter, even swathed in a heavy topcoat, is painful just to contemplate. Bolton was the first town in the area to introduce motor buses onto its streets. The first was a steam powered Stirling that ran on the route from Darcy Lever to Brownlow Fold in 1904. This was augmented by a Darracq-Serpollet model that was introduced in 1907. However, this latter vehicle proved to be unsuccessful and was subsequently replaced in 1908 by a Commer and a Straker petrol-electric. Municipal transport began in the town in the 1880s when horse-drawn trams were introduced. These were in turn replaced by electric trams and the motor bus had to wait until the 1920s before it really mounted a challenge for supremacy. By 1927 a series of express bus routes were established to neighbouring places such as Salford, Wigan and Warrington. The expanding fleet was housed in a new garage, built in 1929 on Crook Street. Then, trolley buses came along and, by taking over some of the tram routes, helped to precipitate the demise of that mode of public transport.

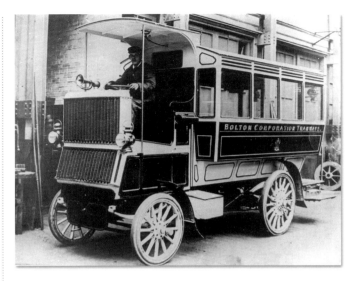

Below: 'Hold on tight, please.' This was the usual instruction offered by the conductor, but in this case he should have been addressing himself as he hung onto the pole on the rear platform of this 1926 Leyland Leviathan. Leyland Motors began life as the Lancashire Steam Motor Company, founded by the Sumner and Spurrier families in 1896, changing its name to incorporate their home town in 1907. Although the company also produced cars, its name became synonymous with the lorries and buses it built in increasing numbers. The Leviathan was just one of a series of public transport vehicles that rolled off the production lines in the 1920s. Other models included the Lion, Lioness, Leveret, Leopard, Titan and Tiger. The bus in view took its name from the great mythical sea monster, said in legend to have been capable of consuming a whale a day. That sounds like the start of a slogan for a chocolate bar, but that one had not been introduced into production when this bus bowled along our streets.

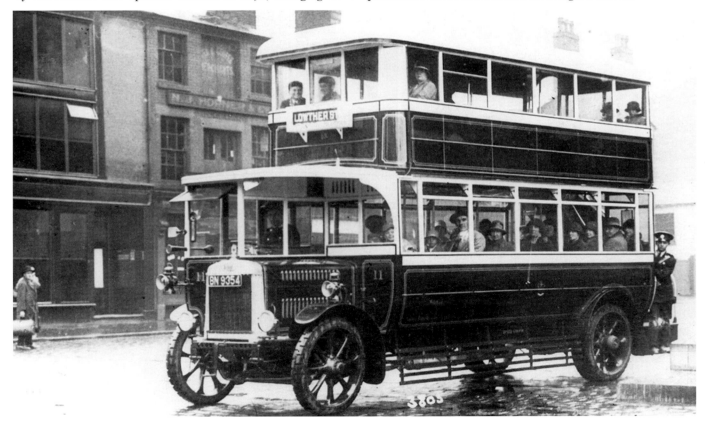

Left: The last tram to run in Bolton was beautifully decorated and its coachwork had been given an extra buffing on this poignant day. It marked the end of an era for public transport in the town. Electric trams had been running for nearly half a century, but on Saturday 29 March 1947, it all came to an end as the No 440 took the Tonge Moor route for the very last time. Somewhat ironically, Bolton's Coat of Arms includes the motto 'Supera Moras'. This translates as 'overcome delays' and is a fitting epitaph to a vehicle and system that served the township well. The first decade after the last war saw many towns and cities abandon their tramlines and go completely over to the motor bus, having a flirtation with trolley buses on the way in some instances. How strange it is that a modern city like Manchester has reintroduced the tram, running services out of town as far afield as Altrincham and Bury. In addition, some other satellite towns around the city that have not been included, for example Rochdale, have complained bitterly about their exclusion. In the current climate of rising fuel costs and restrictions on exhaust omissions, perhaps we phased out the wrong form of transport. We can only guess what would have happened if the bus had been abandoned and the tram system expanded, instead of the other way round.

Below: The Vulcan van had come a cropper and the traffic policeman, possibly a motor cyclist to tell from his boots, was making a careful entry into his notebook. In time, he might have to inform the 'beak' on the bench that he was proceeding in a westerly direction when he came upon the scene that confronted him, or words to that effect. As usual, whenever there is any form of road traffic accident, a small crowd of onlookers had stopped to gawp. Quite what was so fascinating that led one man to examine the front axle with such interest is difficult to determine. The shops in the background are from a bygone age when there was a multitude of individual retail outlets on our streets, all complementing one another as they looked for our trade. The baker and confectioner sold Daren bread that probably came from Feltwell's Tower Mill in Norfolk. It was advertised as being 'best for health', which was a fairly simple slogan compared with some of the more gimmicky ones that modern admen use. Further along, Peacock's tobacconist had a traditional selection of cigarettes to sell. Woodbines were commonly known as 'coffin nails', for obvious reasons. Craven A, an early filter tipped variety, tried to suggest that its product was beneficial by stating that you should smoke this brand 'for your throat's sake'. Get that one past the advertising standards people in this day and age!

Above: Remember when we had proper winters with snow on the ground and cars slipping as the tyres tried to get a grip in the slush on the roads? Is it an illusion, or does it seem to us that young children have had little opportunity to build a snowman these days? Global warming certainly appears to have changed things because those of us who have been on this planet for some time can well recall long spells of wintry weather when we walked to school as the buses were not running and we made death defying slides in the icy playgrounds before the caretaker spoiled our fun by tipping salt onto ground. Something else has changed as well since this photograph of a motorist filling up with petrol at Belmont in 1961. Petrol was 4s 7d a gallon. That is 23p in modern parlance, or about 5p a litre if you want to be completely modern about things. That was for the Super grade; Regular was even cheaper. What a mind boggling statistic that is when you compare it with the price on the forecourts today. Successive hikes in the cost of fuel tax, as well as increased tariffs charged by suppliers, make us long for the days when it cost less than a couple of quid to fill the tank. Not only do we have to fork out a wallet full of cash, we also have to dispense the petrol ourselves. That's progress.

Above: Standing on the Johnson Street footbridge as the steam locomotives made their way into Trinity Street Station was a trainspotters' paradise in the early 1960s. Little lads, their notebooks and pencils in their hands, dutifully recorded the numbers of every engine that rolled past. Some bought dedicated books that had the unique numbers of all the British locos and they crossed off each one they had seen. Most gave up their hobby as the teenage attractions of football, girls and the pub beckoned, but others continued their interest, though it was never quite the same when the boilers stopped chuffing out steam. Hanging over the footbridge, enveloped in white clouds, was a special feeling that could not be reproduced by any newfangled diesel-electric. True railway enthusiasts developed their own language and spoke of slugs, gronks and rats. To the uninitiated, these were different types of locomotive classes. Of course, any true trainspotter was equipped with more than book and pencil. A Thermos flask and a bag of sandwiches were essential because of the long hours spent on platforms and bridges. In wet and windy conditions it was also a good idea to wear, dare we mention the words, an anorak. This bridge closed in 1980, taking many memories with it.

Below: The wheels came off the railway industry in the 1960s, though not as literally as in the case of this locomotive that jumped the track at Bridgeman Street in May 1961. This was the beginning of the era of the Beeching axe, when branch lines and smaller stations disappeared from the network that had served Britain for well over a century since the Rocket completed its famous trial at Rainhill. Richard Beeching (1913-85) was appointed by the Minister of Transport, Ernest Marples, to the post of chairman of the British Railways Board in 1961. He published a report entitled 'The Reshaping of British Railways'. In it he called for the closure of one-third of the country's 7,000 railway stations. Passenger services would be withdrawn from around 5,000 route miles, thus yielding, a net saving of £18 million per year. The reshaping would also involve the shedding of around 70,000 British Railways jobs over three years. Not surprisingly, the Labour Party, trades unions and the general public objected vehemently, but many of his proposals were pushed through. We can still see the ghosts of old lines and stations today as we stroll around the countryside as many of the tracks that once supported railways have now become cycle paths and ramblers' routes.

Left: If you happen to see a group of grey haired pensioners making their way up to Rivington Pike or setting off to the Trough of Bowland, Leki sticks at the ready, then they just might have been on the platform in Trinity Street Station at Easter 1962. These young ramblers were heading for the hills, haversacks laden with waterproofs, a compass and a spare set of socks nestling alongside their sandwiches. Perhaps they were sixthformers or members of a youth club, but whatever the group dynamics you can be sure that their interest in the open air was something that would have stayed with them for life. Nowadays, they might be members of the Ramblers' Association or perhaps just enthusiasts who meet up as a group of friends to stride out and enjoy the wonderful British countryside. When these young people were photographed, they were part of a generation that had survived and flourished despite wartime rationing and the austerity of the 1950s. These were the teenagers who would set the note for the swinging 60s and make their special bid for recognition as a powerful force in society. They would buck the trends and set new standards of morality and behaviour. Looking back, do they now peer through their spectacles and scratch their balding heads and wonder if it all went to plan?

ROYAL VISITS

When King George VI and Queen Elizabeth visited Bolton in March 1945, the war was nearly won. The big three leaders of the Allies, Stalin, Roosevelt and Churchill, had just met at Yalta to determine the carving up of Europe after Germany had been defeated. Dresden had been obliterated in a devastating air raid and our troops crossed the Rhine and prepared to march on Berlin. By the end of the next month, both Hitler and Mussolini would be dead. So, it was a confidently joyous crowd that watched the royal couple on the Town Hall steps where they were accompanied by Mayor Walter Bradley, the owner of an engineering firm based on Deansgate. He had represented the Tonge Moor ward since 1921. Queen Elizabeth was one of the most popular members of the royal family that we have ever had, even if she only qualified via her marriage to the former Duke of York, Prince Albert. As Elizabeth Bowes-Lyon, she was one of Britain's most attractive young ladies in high society. Even so, she baulked at first at the idea of becoming a royal when Albert proposed. However, she was won over, partly because she realised that her prospective husband would only have a peripheral role in the monarchy as his brother, the Prince of Wales and his future offspring, would succeed to the throne. How wrong she was, as the abdication crisis of 1936 was to prove.

Above: The mighty motorcade swept along Trinity Street, Bradshawgate, Great Moor Street and Newport Street on 22 October, 1954. It had collected Queen Elizabeth and the Duke of Edinburgh from the royal train and conveyed the special guests of honour, together with a variety of attendants, to the Town Hall. Despite being an atrocious day, with the rain coming down in torrents at times, people turned out in their thousands. Children waved little Union flags on sticks and cheered for all they were worth. Royalty was something to be respected and admired in those days and we were proud to celebrate our monarchy. We did not want a republic like France or Germany and certainly not a dictatorship such as the USSR offered. The British had their special way of doing things and having a king or queen as head of state served us very well, thank you. The royals were on a two day visit to Lancashire and, in the days when televisions were not a commonplace item in every front room, this was one of the few opportunities that we had to see our monarch at close quarters. When the visitors left the parish church bells rang out in celebration of the honour that had been paid by this visit to our humble, northern town.

The cameraman had a difficult job trying to get a snap of Queen Elizabeth II and her entourage as they drove along the town centre streets in October 1954. People stood on tiptoe to get a better look at Her Majesty, but in truth it would have been the most fleeting of glimpses. Still, they went home happy in the knowledge that they had done their patriotic bit in turning out to cheer themselves hoarse. The throng in Victoria Square was royally entertained by a band before the royal guests made their entry. Some had been standing patiently for several hours so that they could claim a front row view on the pavement. As the Queen turned her head and smiled it seemed as if it was a personal hello to each and every subject who had ventured out. When she left her car a special look and gesture was made to a group of limbless ex-servicemen who were seated by the Town Hall steps.

Above: Part of the duties of a colonel-in-chief is to carry out an inspection of the troops. The Queen did this during her 1954 visit as she carefully checked the Guard of Honour lined up for her. The eagle-eyed spotted a diamond and pearl badge of the Loyal Regiment on her lapel that had been presented to her the previous year. When Princess Elizabeth succeeded her father in 1952 it came as something of a surprise. Although he had been in poor health of late, his death was so unexpected that his heir was on holiday in Kenya and was intending to fly on to Australia. She was given the bad news that he had passed away at Sandringham and returned immediately to London. Elizabeth was just 25 and the youngest to succeed to the throne since her great-great grandmother, Victoria. Although the nation mourned the loss of a king, many viewed Elizabeth's accession as a symbol of a new Elizabethan age. We were recovering from the war and its aftermath and, perhaps, we could now move on apace as the second half of the 20th century unfolded.

Right: She had only been on the throne for two years when Queen Elizabeth II made a visit to our town. Seen here with the Lord Mayor, Peter Flanagan, she cut a dashing figure. Still in her 20s, she had a winning smile that could melt a few hearts. Her escort was a man who had risen from the humblest of roots. Peter Flanagan (1897-1964) was the sixth of ten children. He attended Albert Place School and by the turn of the century was working halftime at Charnock's Ropewalk. A ropewalk is a long, straight, narrow lane, or covered pathway, where long strands of material were laid before being twisted into rope. These places were often notoriously harsh sweatshops that frequently caught on fire as hemp dust formed an explosive mixture. Flanagan certainly came up the hard way. He would later work for a tobacconist, a blacksmith and in a foundry before taking a post at the Bolton Workshop for the Blind. His tough upbringing made him keen to help improve the lot of the working classes. As a committed trades union member he held senior positions in the branch office of the Gas Workers and General Labourers' Union. He turned to local politics in 1933, winning a council seat representing the Rumworth ward, a position he held for 30 years. During his mayoral year he met many famous visitors as well as Queen Elizabeth. Sir Jacob Epstein, Sir Thomas Beecham, Lady Isobel Barnett and Sir Billy Butlin were all received by him. He even danced with actress Googie Withers at the Mayor's Ball, stating that this was one perk of the office that he thoroughly enjoyed.

Left: Second children are almost always more feisty than their elder siblings. This is hardly surprising as they have to battle with their elders for recognition and attention. Princess Margaret Rose was no exception. Born in 1930, her elder sister, the future Queen Elizabeth II, was already turned four and was the apple of her parents' eye. Needless to say, Margaret had to make her own mark on life and her parents' affections in a determined manner from the word go. The girls were privately educated by the royal nanny, Marion Crawford or 'Crawfie' as they called her. Whilst Elizabeth was a well behaved youngster, Crawfie always found Margaret a handful. After the war, Margaret moved in society circles and was regarded as one of the most beautiful young women on the scene. She enjoyed the party life and the trappings that went with it. However, lasting happiness was always elusive. In the early 1950s she met Peter Townsend, a member of the Royal Household and a former Battle of Britain ace. They fell in love, but their hopes of marriage were doomed. He was a divorced man and a commoner. With shades of her uncle's abdication dilemma in 1936, Margaret decided to end the affair officially in late 1955. In 1960 she married Anthony Armstrong-Jones and had two children by him. She looked happy enough in 1967 when she made an official visit to open the Octagon Theatre, receiving a silver water jug from JR Townson, representing the contractors under the gaze of Alderman CH Lucas, but she was to live out her later years as a troubled, lonely woman.

Above: Commentators have sometimes been rather unkind to Princess Anne, but no one can criticise her determination and interest in the lot of others. In her own right, she became an international sportswoman. As an equestrian, she won a number of major titles and represented her country at the 1976 Montreal Olympics. She and daughter Zara have the unique record of both being elected BBC Sports Personality of the Year, in 1971 and 2006 respectively. Her selfless charity work has taken her across the globe, particularly to poverty stricken African nations. Anne showed her particular strength of character during a most unpleasant and frightening incident in 1974. She was travelling with her first husband, Mark Phillips, in her chauffeur driven limousine along London's Pall Mall when an armed assailant tried to kidnap her. When told to get out of the car, she responded in typical fashion by responding 'Not b***** likely!' The man was overpowered, though several others were injured in the melee. She was still a teenager when she represented her mother in a visit to a Bolton mill in 1969. Here she shakes hands with KN Patel, watched by co-workers Margaret Farrell and Terence Daly. In 1987, Anne was awarded the title of Princess Royal, becoming the seventh person to be so honoured.

WORKING LIFE

The skyline of bygone Bolton shows what a mucky place it once was. Numerous factory chimneys belched out their noxious fumes into the air, but we could not have done without them. They provided much of the town's economy and we all know the saying about beggars and choosers. Those were the days when a shirt or blouse only lasted a few hours before becoming covered with black flecks and collars and cuffs were grimy well before the end of the day. It was not until after the last war that various Clean Air Acts were passed in an effort to reduce the level of pollution, but even those only had limited effect until the mills finally declined. This view was taken from Queen's Park Terrace and also shows chimneys that belonged to Bessemer's Forge that was in operation until 1924. It later became the site of the Moor Lane car park. The prominent chimney in the centre belonged to Jackson's flour mill.

Piled high with tempting produce, the Market Hall had everything that a shopper seeking to stock the family larder could desire. Building began in 1854 and the hall first opened for business on 19 December, 1855, at a cost of £50,000. At nearly 300 feet in length and covering an area of 7,000 square yards, it was said to be 'the largest covered market in the kingdom'.

A long procession marked the opening ceremony of this magnificent building. It continued to serve the public until well into this century before being closed for redevelopment, despite howls of protest from those who wanted to see the Grade II listed building preserved in as close a manner to its Victorian roots as possible. Bolton has a long heritage as a bustling market town. In 1251 Henry III granted the town a Royal Charter to hold a market in the manor of Bowelton every seventh day and to hold a three-day fair at the same place once a year. The first 19th century markets were held close to the Parish Church, Churchgate, and in New Market Place between 1826 and 1871.

Above: It was all switches, plugs, jacks and cables in the Post Office Telephone Exchange with not a fibre-optic or silicon chip in sight. A mobile was something you hung above the baby's cot to give the little one something to watch instead of howling the place down and broadband was an adornment to a schoolgirl's panama hat. Telephone operators had an important role to fulfil. Before the days of dial-up telephones, they would be act as the third party who connected a caller to the recipient. Those of us with long memories can recall that smaller exchanges would have only a tiny handful of operators who always seemed very well informed about everyone else's business. Being able to eavesdrop on a so-called private conversation was very useful for the village gossip. Younger readers will not remember the old public telephones we used to have, with their Button A to connect or Button B to get your money back. Every kiddie worth his salt nipped into a box before going past in order to press that letter B button. Every so often there was a reward awaiting the fortunate child, thanks to a forgetful previous caller. In this photograph, two supervisors were keeping a very careful check on the way the exclusively female staff were carrying out their duties. It is just as well that the merriment on the face of the young woman in the foreground went unnoticed.

Below: The age of steam for Horwich Locomotive Works came to an end with the departure of the last engine on 6 May, 1964. Number 48756 was not the last word for the yard as it continued to handle rolling stock until 1983, but it was definitely the start of the final chapter. The Lancashire and Yorkshire Railway originally opened a works at Gorton, Manchester, but the site could not be extended sufficiently to cope with the company's growth. A new home was found in Horwich in 1886 and soon expanded to become the town's main employer. The first locomotive built here was a 2-4-2 tank engine, completed in 1889. Designed by John Aspinall, it is now preserved in the National Railway Museum. Aspinall was responsible for the production of an impressive 677 locomotives in a decade. It really was a hotbed of industry, averaging better than one locomotive per week. In 1923 the L&YR became part of the London Midland Scottish company and, with George Hughes as the chief mechanical engineer, built the very successful 'Horwich Crab' series that served well into the 1960s. Nigel Gresley, perhaps the most famous name in steam locomotive design, was once employed here in a senior capacity. The final steam engine, a class 4-6-0, was produced in 1957, though a number of diesel shunters were built at Horwich until 1962.

who could earn 30 shillings a week, quite a tidy sum at the time. However, this was to change with the introduction of the power loom. Invented by the Reverend Edmund Cartwright in 1785, it was faster and more economical than the handloom. As it could be operated by young, untrained hands who were willing to work for a pittance, the well paid days of the handloom worker were gone. As the machinery improved and the number of factories grew, efficiency and competition forced prices ever lower and men and women worked long hours for scant reward. By the time we reached the 20th century, conditions had improved considerably. Even so, the work was still tiring and not particularly well remunerated. There was also a boredom factor of doing such repetitive work, as these women hemming towels would testify. Despite a working environment that was healthier than that endured by their grandparents, the women in the photograph still carried out their jobs in old, draughty buildings with just 'Workers' Playtime' on the radio tannoy to keep them cheerful. Although most of the 'dark, satanic mills' have now been pulled down or turned into flats, they live on as part of our heritage.

Above: This was the sort of scene that inspired LS Lowry's artwork, with his matchstalk men, cats and dogs. Workers leaving the mill at the end of a shift, making their way across the cobbled setts, were part of the scene that once epitomised every mill town in the north of England. The textile trade was little more than a cottage industry until the Industrial Revolution sprang into life. In the 18th century, such inventions as Kay's flying shuttle, Hargreaves' spinning jenny, Crompton's spinning mule and Cartwright's power loom revolutionised this field. They helped provide the tools for mass production and the explosion in the building of large mills that could employ huge workforces and turn out massive amounts of cotton, wool and silk fabric every day. Bolton's involvement with textiles was influenced by Flemish weavers who settled here in the 14th century. They also introduced clog making. This footwear was almost compulsory for workers at one time. The sparks fairly flew from their feet as they made their way to and from their place of employment. Wool was the most common commodity at first as cotton was not introduced until the 17th century. Bolton's first spinning mill was built in 1780.

Right: New types of looms and shuttles increased the productivity of the textile industry in the late 18th century. A skilled handloom operator was a valued employee

Rivington Taylor - Delving for Furniture

When Bolton's Rivington Taylor store in Manchester Road was opened by Mark and Alison Haslam the event was not just something new, but the culmination of a whole century of family enterprise. With 40,000 square feet of showroom dedicated solely to home furnishings, not only is Rivington Taylor Bolton's largest furniture showroom, but also one of the largest such stores in the North of England.

When Mark Haslam's great grandfather, Thomas Taylor, first started a quarrying business at Montcliffe, Rivington on the moors above Bolton almost 100 years ago, he could not have realised that his legacy would live on well into the 21st century.

Thomas Taylor founded his business, working literally with his bare hands. The firm became a hugely successful enterprise, supplying stone nationwide, including that used for many of Manchester's pavements.

But family roots in Bolton go back even further. Mark Haslam's great great grandfather, John Scholes, played football for the very first Bolton Wanderers side back in the 1880s when the team was called Pikes Lane FC. Now in the 21st century Mark Haslam is the proud possessor of the football medals won by his illustrious ancestor, medals

which are safety stored in the bank for posterity. Today Rivington Taylor remains a family business. And its priority is what you would expect from a business that believes its single most valuable asset is its reputation.

Old fashioned customer service is fundamental to the firm's values in the family's latest business venture, run by Mark Haslam and his wife Alison. Real service is something Rivington Taylor staff strive to achieve in every aspect of customers' experience - from the moment customers walk over the store's threshold to when furniture and furnishings are safely delivered to their homes.

All the major quality branded furniture, crafted by the best manufacturers from Britain, France, Germany and, of course, Italy are in stock. Having such a large showroom however, the firm also has room to offer pieces from the far-flung corners of the world, enabling Rivington Taylor to offer both products that are truly unique, hand finished pieces, as well as competitively priced imported items.

Top left: *A Taylor family photograph with Thomas Taylor in the centre back row.* **Above and below:** *Interior and exterior views of the Rivington Taylor showroom.*

Astley Dye & Chemical Co. Ltd - The Story of Acdo

The Astley Dye & Chemical Co Ltd, often better known locally simply as Acdo, has always been based in Bolton. It has been a major employer in the town for generations, with many examples of employees spending their entire working lives in the business, sometimes including many members of the same families.

Today the business remains committed to a future in Bolton, and to retaining the excellent standing it enjoys within the community – a community it has been part of since the early decades of the 20th century.

Above: Founder, Harry Pilling. **Below:** *An early horse drawn 'A' board used to publicise Acdo demonstrations by Harry Pilling and his mother.* **Right:** *The packaging line at the company's new Mallison Street factory in 1928. The Acdotablets were wrapped in greaseproof paper before being labelled and stacked ready for despatch.*

Not long after the end of the Great War, Harry Pilling was a young office boy working in a chemical company based in Bolton. Even though he was only just out of school Harry had strong ambitions and saw himself as the main breadwinner for his family, a feeling that was brought on by the fact that Harry had lost his father as a young boy. So at the early age of sixteen Harry Pilling decided that the best way to make his fortune was to set up his own business; and that is exactly what he did when in 1919 he founded what would become the Astley Dye and Chemical Company – and ACDO was born.

The idea which inspired the young Harry Pilling was based on a 'miracle' product to help alleviate the drudgery that the 1920s housewife faced with her weekly wash. In those days washing was a chore dreaded by most housewives, with only a washboard, mangle and ordinary household soap to help ease the burden.

The product that Harry Pilling developed – ACDO – was initially sold in the form of a solid tablet. The essential ingredient of the Acdo Washing Tablet was sodium perborate, a remarkable chemical product that Harry Pilling had encountered on a working trip to Germany.

A process for manufacturing the miracle additive to soap had been developed in 1903 by Frenchman George François Jaubert, but the manufacturing process had only recently been perfected by a German chemist named Otto Liebknecht.

Adding this wonder ingredient to soap meant that Acdo took all the hard work of rubbing and scrubbing out of the wash, with its remarkable ability to remove stains and add 'detergency'.

Today most forward thinking businesses recognise the importance of 'image', promotions and marketing. In the 1920s this wasn't always the case. Bearing that in mind, the young Harry

Pilling's ability to use innovative ways of selling Acdo was impressive - especially from one so young and inexperienced in the world of business.

Several aspects of the way that Acdo was promoted bear witness to Harry's abilities; initially the solid Acdo tablet needed to be grated into water, so free graters were offered to housewives who sent in Acdo wrappers. Harry also firmly believed in taking the Acdo message directly to where his customers were likely to be found. To that end he organised free demonstrations in local church halls and schools, inviting housewives to come and bring their washing with them, offering free teas to those who attended. Bolton housewives came along in their hundreds to witness Harry's mother washing their clothes with Acdo, and to hear Harry's sales talk. The result was that sales grew strongly by word of mouth as news of the time-saving miracle washing product spread.

Top left: One of Acdo's early delivery vehicles. Top right: Pictured in 1938 alongside their liveried van are the mobile sales team for the north east of England. Left: A 1934 Acdo exhibition stand. The posters proclaim Acdo as the 'twenty minute washer'. These demonstrations held by Harry and his mother were attended by hundreds of Bolton housewives.

In the mid to late 1950s the growing popularity of television prompted Harry Pilling to experiment with TV advertising. Yet again his knack for knowing how to promote his product was invaluable in recognising the potential that broadcasting the Acdo message into households

When starting the business in 1919 Harry Pilling and his mother initially produced the washing tablets in their kitchen. Using a mixing bowl and spoon the soap was blended rolled out and cut into squares before drying. It was then wrapped in greaseproof paper and labelled. Gradually the success of Harry's

demonstrations and other sales tactics meant the popularity of Acdo grew, with local housewives first buying it themselves and then telling their friends. Eventually demand became so great that the business outgrew the kitchen table and new premises were acquired in Mallinson Street near Astley Bridge. By 1928 demand had grown so great that a night shift had to be employed.

The pricing policy of Acdo in the early years was based on Harry Pilling's commonsense approach to the finances of the business. The 'threepence a tablet' price was, according to Harry himself, a result of applying the simple formula: 'a penny to make, a penny to distribute, and a penny for me'.

Though the 1930s were a grim time for many, they were a time of progress for Acdo, and in 1938 'Shredded Acdo' was launched, when the long familiar three-ounce solid pack was discontinued and a larger pack introduced containing the same weight but in suet-like particles. It was now possible to use Acdo straight from the pack, making the old graters superfluous.

would have. Success was immediate, and sales of Acdo doubled between 1959 and 1962. By this time Harry's son Marshal Pilling had joined the company working his way up from the factory floor to become Managing Director in 1956.

The second household name brand to come from Acdo was Glo White, introduced in 1957. Glo White very quickly achieved sales success as a product to whiten nylons when added to the wash.

The mid 1970s saw ACDO expand its product range even further in order to meet the constantly increasing expectations of consumers. Glo White Net Curtain Whitener soon established itself as another household name, and the Glo White range quickly demonstrated the innovative approach to product development that had been the hallmark of the firm since its early days.

Top: 1950s Acdo billboard adverising. **Above left:** *All ready to embark on a company outing.* **Below:** *Harry Pilling taking a close interest in the production procces in the 1950s.*

traditional values and the unique benefits of ACDO's vegetable oil soap-based washing powders that had remained strong for so long.

The early 1990s was very much a hand-over period with Chairman Marshall Pilling and his son Brandon working closely together. Harry Pilling had died at the age of 83. The third generation of the Pilling family now ran the business, with two of Marshall Pilling's four children directly involved. Brandon Pilling became Managing Director in 1992, successfully steering the company along a demanding strategic path of growth through new product development, and by nurturing markets at home and overseas.

Advertising continued to play an important role at ACDO and the 1990s saw the re-introduction of the focus on customer care, fronted by Helen Why, the face of the company's customer service team. Helen was to become a key element of the company's publicity, and today she fronts a 'virtual' service bureau on the company's website.

Later still, the introduction of revolutionary porous sachets resembling giant teabags heralded the introduction of Glo White In Wash Stain Remover which was soon followed by its 'teabag' stable mate Glo White In Wash Superwhitener. These convenient no mess products soon caught the imagination of the public in the same way that the Acdo soap block had done seventy years earlier.

By the dawn of the 1990s the Glo White range consisted of eleven different products including Ultra Wash Booster, Rescue Colour Run Remover, Travel Wash, Wonderbar, In Wash Net Curtain Whitener and Glo White In Wash Colour Catcher.

With exports now going to over ten countries the revolution that started on a kitchen table in Bolton had converts all over the world, from Europe, across the Middle East, along the Pacific rim and down to Australia.

The 1990s also saw the launch of ACDO Superwash, and in 1996 Original ACDO, both concentrated machine-wash powders. Original ACDO brought the product full circle, relying on

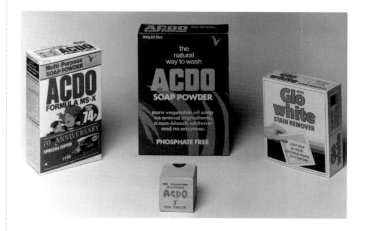

The strength of Glo White as the company's leading brand continued throughout the decade with sales in 'niche' laundry far outselling those of the Acdo brand. However, the most significant event of the 1990s was an alliance formed with German company Delta Pronatura.

Top: Mrs Maude Pilling, wife of Harry, is pictured at an exhibition demonstrating the virtues of using Acdo to actress Jean Kent. Left: A view inside the packaging department in the 1960s. Above: In the 1920s the Acdo soap tablet was the best thing around for washday. The soap tablet needed to be grated into a powder before use. In the 1990s ACDO marketed environmental friendly soap powders and Glo White stain remover, the latter in a porous bag, that you simply popped into the washing machine to remove stains.

Delta Pronatura is a strong international third generation family-owned company which markets and sells its products under the Dr Beckmann and Stain Devils brands and was actively trading in the UK. At the time ACDO was considering launching similar products but felt that partnering with Delta made more sense. The consensus being that, rather than going to the expense of copying, why not use ACDO's expertise in distribution to build a business with Delta.

By the mid 1990s the UK market was becoming static, whilst the demand from certain trade sectors for the ACDO brand declined with the rise of supermarkets. With the static domestic market, exporting became a crucial way to grow the company.

Starting with small markets, such as Cyprus and Malta, business rapidly expanded to the point that a separate Export Department was required. By the end of 2000 exports represented over 20 per cent of the company's laundry additive business, and products were being sold in over 30 countries. As a result of working with its partner Delta, the UK deal soon developed into

an international one, with ACDO representing Delta in certain markets and Delta representing ACDO in others.

The 1990s was a period of partnering and launching many interesting and unique products in the field of laundry and laundry specialists, but also now some specialist household items made an appearance. The final act of diversification in the decade was the acquisition of a local janitorial manufacturer which heralded ACDO's entry into the Professional/Business to Business market sector. As a consequence a final corporate decision was taken to resolve the dichotomy between 'ACDO the manufacturer of products' and 'Acdo the brand name' and in 1999 the company was re-named ACDOCO.

Sadly the new millennium was marked by the death of its then Chairman Marshall Pilling; this now left the company in the sole control of its new Chairman and Managing Director Brandon Pilling.

However, diversification remained still high on the agenda, and 2000 saw the launch of a new strategic alliance with Italian company Coswell to launch specialist personal care items into the U.K. market – initially as a range of aluminium-free deodorants called Bionsen, and later tooth-whitening products under the trademark Blanx.

Top left: *TV presenter Hughie Greene advertising Acdo in the 1970s.* **Left:** *Marshall Pilling with ACDO's then Marketing Director Tony Isbell at the Cool-It launch.* **Above:** *The launch of Original Acdo in 1996.*

focused business trading in specialist laundry care, household care, and personal care.

The business at Astley Bridge continues to manufacture products whilst retaining trading control in the professional and wholesale sectors - and retaining the Acdo brand, Brandon Pilling's legacy from his grandfather.

The year 2009 marks the 90th trading year of the Acdo trademark in the UK. With its centenary in sight the company is a rare example of business longevity in this day and age: its celebration will be a fitting tribute to the Acdo brand.

For the foreseeable future international business will also continue out of the Astley Bridge offices.

International business carried on apace, and ACDOCO made a strategic acquisition in South Africa, buying its distribution partner Mates Beauty and creating a subsidiary that specialised in the personal care market.

With the distribution business expanding, partner business growing, and international business increasing, ACDOCO began to outgrow its premises at Astley Bridge despite extending buildings in every direction.

In 2003 a decision was made to move warehousing and distribution to Blackburn, effectively splitting the company into a manufacturing unit at the original premises in Astley Bridge and a dedicated distribution centre at its offices in Mill Hill in Blackburn.

The following years saw the company grow and invest heavily in a market dominated by the retail giants. The need to be a bigger company with ever more critical mass became the focus for that period of time, in turn stimulating an ever-greater focus on the need for new product development and innovation.

And all these activities will take place under the watchfull eye of the original corporate structure which remains firmly in the grip of family control under the chairmanship of Brandon Pilling, and now appropriately re-named as the Astley Dye & Chemical Co. Limited.

Top left: Bolton Tram Car Number 66 proudly displays it's Acdo branding celebrating the company's 75th anniversary.
Below left: Acdo products from the twenties to the seventies carrying the slogan 'Still washes whitest and brightest'.
Above: Professional Products. *Below:* Three generations of the Pilling family: Marshall (left), Brandon (centre), and David (right), in front of the portrait of Harry, founder of the company.

In 2007 a significant decision was made to formalise the strategic partnership with Delta Pronatura, and to also formalise the now re-structured UK business to ensure that it continued to grow and remain successful. Brandon Pilling very much saw the need for the company to be part of a European-wide structure, rather than operating in the UK in isolation. In 2007 the commercial business at Blackburn was officially partnered by Delta and 'new ACDOCO' was launched as a UK-

Prestons Of Bolton - The Diamond Centre of the North

just half past ten

Every Christmas children and their parents visit the Edwardian Christmas grotto on the third floor at Prestons of Bolton to meet Santa. All good children receive a present, whilst their parents are refreshed with a soft drink, or something a little stronger.

Though the youngsters may be thrilled at the prospect of toys for Christmas it's a fair bet that the adults will have in mind something more enduring than dolls and bags of sweets: though most Christmas presents are short-lived, diamonds are forever.

Ask almost anyone over the age of 35 born and brought up in the North West of England to name a jewellery store and they will almost invariably name Prestons of Bolton. In the 1970s and 1980s the company became the largest supplier of diamond engagement rings from a single store in the whole of the United Kingdom.

Prestons of Bolton has over the years supplied more diamond engagement rings and wedding rings than any other store in the UK.

The landmark Bolton building has three floors dedicated to the finest collection of diamond rings, wedding rings, jewellery, wrist watches and giftware.

The name of Prestons has long been known throughout the North of England as the leading independent jewellers in the region. But the Prestons that would become a

business with branches in many parts of the country began in the 19th century in Victorian Bolton when watchmaker James Preston first opened for business.

Master Jeweller James Preston began selling watches and jewellery in Bolton in 1869. The town was enjoying the relative prosperity that the industrial revolution and the booming cotton trade had brought.

Prestons first shop was in Bank Street, Bolton, and soon gained a reputation for high quality and fair dealing.

Top left: *Just half past ten, this rakish looking gentleman lighting up his cigarette while checking the time from the light of his match, featured on the front cover of Prestons watch brochure in 1937.* ***Below left and below:*** *The invitation to the opening of Prestons new premises in 1913. The invitation unfolded to reveal the royal likeness between Queen Victoria, Edward VII and King George V.*

THE GREATEST EVENT IN BOLTON'S HISTORY
Will be the
Royal Visit on July 10th, 1913.

THE
NEXT GREATEST EVENT
will be the OPENING of the Largest Jewellery Establishment in the North of England, on JULY 24th, 1913, by
PRESTONS LTD.
BOLTON'S FOREMOST JEWELLERS.
Deansgate and Bank St., Bolton.

The Royal Likeness

Business prospered and the impressive premises at Deansgate in the centre of Bolton were acquired and developed in 1904. In 1912 the original building was demolished and a newer, larger, purpose-built store was opened in 1913. The invitation to the opening rather less-than-modestly described the opening as the second most important event in Bolton's history, the first being the visit by King George V only two weeks earlier. When it opened the store was the largest of its kind in England, and it still is.

At the start of the 20th century Prestons had already forged a reputation as one of the most comprehensive and prestigious jewellers in England, with customers coming to Bolton from many other parts of the country: word of mouth being the major medium for the business to attract new customers.

Company founder James Preston died in 1905 leaving Gertrude Sheppard to run the business. Gertrude, great aunt of the subsequent Managing Director, Andrew Duckworth, had been working for James Preston since the age of fourteen.

By 1920, Gertrude Sheppard had acquired a controlling interest in the company and from that time Prestons would be a family run business with her relatives the Duckworths. In 1949 Gordon Duckworth joined the firm.

Prestons had continued to build on its reputation as Britain's premier jewellers outside London. By the 1950s Gordon Duckworth had taken up the reins. Realising that demand for jewellery was continuing to grow in the post-war economic boom, Gordon Duckworth soon began a phase of expansion which saw Prestons open a branch in Leigh, among others locations.

The Leigh branch was an immediate success and Prestons was able to consolidate its position throughout the 1960s, operating from a number of outlets. Gordon Duckworth's son Andrew joined Prestons in 1972 and shortly after this a new marketing tactic saw Prestons become the first jewellery retailer in the country to advertise on television.

Advertising on Granada Television and in cinemas throughout the country was a stroke of genius. The most

Above: Early advertising. Below: A view inside the silver showroom of the 1960s.

famous advert was shot on location in New York City and featured a couple walking hand in hand through Times Square, their gaze wanders upward where, lit up on the electronic billboard, is the name 'Prestons of Bolton'. The phrase 'It's always worth a journey to the Diamond Centre of the North' helped build a legendary business.

Using the medium of television for Prestons' advertising was to be a major factor in the company's growth over the following fifteen years. The various advertising campaigns during the seventies and eighties established Prestons as 'The Diamond Centre of the North - Prestons of Bolton', the phrase that many people still use to describe the company.

The firm's visitors book from the 1970s and 1980s shows that couples travelled from all over the United Kingdom; on one single Saturday in 1975 Prestons of Bolton sold no fewer than 169 wedding rings. Indeed, on Saturdays the Bolton store was often so busy that customers had to queue with a ticket until their number was called to be seen by a sales person.

Andrew Duckworth became Managing Director of Prestons in 1980, with Gordon Duckworth becoming Chairman. In subsequent years Prestons undertook a planned expansion that saw it open branches outside its traditional northern base. Outlets opened in York, Guildford and Windsor. A watch concession opened in the House of Fraser store in Birmingham as well as other concessions in Altrincham and Wilmslow.

Gordon Duckworth retired in 1990 and his son Andrew became Managing Director.

In 1994 Prestons acquired Croydons - another independent jeweller with two outlets in Bury St. Edmunds and Ipswich in Suffolk. Prestons' first outlet in Scotland appeared with its watch concession in Jenners department store, Edinburgh.

Top: *The Queen passes Prestons on her 1968 visit to Bolton.*
Above: *The gift department in 1996.*

Meanwhile the 'family run feel' remained strong, and Andrew Duckworth's brother Quentin played a key role as the Director responsible for sales and marketing. A third Duckworth brother, Neil, took an interest, but initially not in a direct role as he had his own successful business.

In 2002 Neil Duckworth took over the business which was now re-branded Preston and Duckworth Ltd, reflecting the long period of time that the Duckworth family had been involved with the firm.

Re-branding was not, however, the complete success that had been hoped for, and in 2005 the firm was sold to Cottrills, another independent jewellery business.

Cottrills, which has jewellery stores in Bramhall, Macclesfield, and Wilmslow was established in 1910 and specialises in handmade diamond jewellery, wedding rings and is one of the leading watch specialists in the North West.

Prestons in Bolton was now closed down prior to a full and sympathetic refurbishment. The last major refit at the store had been in the 1960s, with further work carried out in the 1980s and 1990s. The refit was carried out by award-winning designer Peter Dooley. Over a period of nine months he and his team gutted the building prior to recreating the original mahogany splendour of the Edwardian masterpiece. The store reopened for business in November, 2006, reverting to its original name, Prestons of Bolton.

When it opened in 1913 the Prestons of Bolton building featured one of the few time balls in the country. Situated atop the buildings' clock tower the ball dropped each day when a signal was received from Greenwich at 10 am. By 2001 the structure had become unstable, and to the dismay of the local community the time ball was removed. The restoration of the time ball and its renewed ability to drop in conjunction with the other time ball at Greenwich would be a key objective in 2008.

Looking towards the future, the plan is to keep growing but at a rate which enables the company to choose the right store in the right town, and to enable its legendary levels of customer care and market knowledge to be maintained at the levels that Prestons' customers have come to expect since the firm was founded in the 19th century.

Today Prestons of Bolton is once more a success, and regaining its reputation as the destination store for diamond engagement rings. It is one of only three jewellery stores in Britain to have a bespoke Rolex Room designed and fitted by Rolex-appointed architects; the other two are Harrods and Selfridges in London.

Though much may have changed down the years one thing that has not altered at Prestons is the impeccable standards of service, choice and value for money that are always on offer. With innovative marketing and a reputation extending back to 1869 Prestons of Bolton continues to serve the people of Bolton and far beyond.

The future is sparkling for the Diamond Centre of the North.

Left: The Rolex room at Prestons of Bolton. Below: The compass always points north on the first floor where customers can enjoy a coffee or glass of champagne.

MBDA UK Ltd - Flying High

Though its corporate existence goes back only to 2001 the story of MBDA at Lostock has its origins in the very early years of the 20th century. Geoffrey de Havilland was one of the great pioneers of aircraft design and production of the first half of the twentieth century. The aeroplane manufacturer of pre-World War I days offered pilot training in the same way that car makers ran courses for chauffeurs. During the First World War De Havilland bombers, and many of the pilots trained by the company, would play a vital role.

Two dozen DH9As and ten other aircraft evacuated the Afghan royal household and the entire British diplomatic community from trouble-torn Kabul in late 1928. This classic use of air power occurred in the middle of the inter-war deterioration of aircraft supplies when the armed services were starved of funding. Better known to the 'air minded' public of the era were the well publicised air races and record-breaking flights.

The first de Havilland Comet was a graceful futuristic machine built of wood for the 1934 MacRobertson Air Race between

Above: The MBDA site in May 1957, when the company was known as De Havilland Propellers Limited. Below: Inside the factory staff are hard at work in 1961. Everyone here is highly focused without being distracted by their photograph being taken.

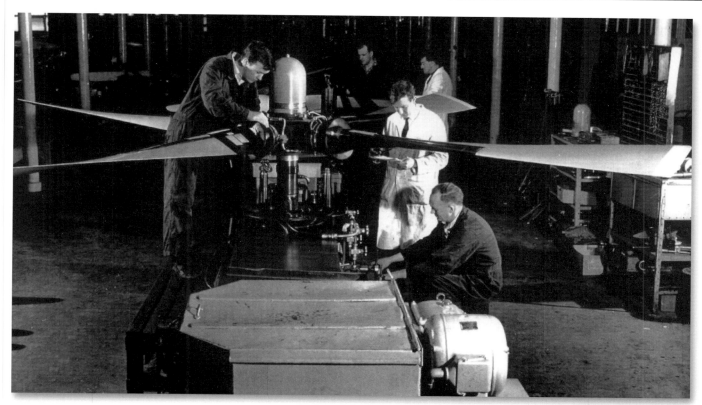

London and Melbourne. She completed the 11,300 miles in seventy-two hours. From this classic design was developed the wartime Mosquito nicknamed the 'Wooden Wonder'.

In 1936 the de Havilland Airscrew Company was established by the parent company at the Garside Street Works in Bolton. A year later a new factory was built at Lostock to house nine hundred employees making propellers. The Lostock site had previously hosted Sir Alan Cobham's famous 'National Aviation Days'. Later Jim Mollison's Gypsy Moth, of the Australian record flight, and the Fox Moth which won the 1932 King's Cup Race were displayed there. Sir Alan had once walked away from a crash in Ainsworth Lane, Bolton, following a short flight from Lostock.

On 15th July 1938 the Lostock factory was officially opened by Sir Thomas Inskip, Minister for Co-ordination of Defence. By now the nation had woken up to the Nazi menace, and by the outbreak of war in September 1939 some ten thousand propellers had been made for twenty aircraft types.

Lostock worked night and day producing and repairing propellers and ancillary equipment during World War II. This valuable site was protected by a battery of 4.5 inch anti-aircraft guns located on the left of Alexandra Road, twin Lewis machine guns on the gatehouse roof and Hispano anti-tank guns in each of the two pill boxes. Additionally smudge pots were located along Chorley New Road which could blanket the entire works with black smoke to frustrate enemy bomb aimers who needed to see their target.

The Home Guard, commanded by Major H Morton, retd, were trained to deal with the incendiary bombs which never came. Although the Luftwaffe had photographed the site in 1941 the nearest bomb damage was opposite the Rumworth Hotel on Wigan Road. Even so, a fleet of lorries took vital blade forgings to dispersal units every night of the war to ensure a reserve in case of air raids. The site of what became West Block was a lorry park for the company's Queen Marys, sixty-foot aircraft transporters that were then the longest vehicles on the road.

Petrol was severely rationed, and although cars were rare only a few key workers received petrol coupons. Most people walked, cycled or took the tram to work and ate in the canteen, where meat pie, mash and gravy for a 'tanner', (6d or 2.5p), was the staple offering.

Office clerks were paid eighteen shillings, (90p), for a five and a half day week. Production workers, with ample overtime, earned considerably more than this. In 1941 de Havilland laid on its first Family Day with a 'bunfight' and stalls in the canteen.

In the early post-war years de Havilland, and other British manufacturers, worked all out, both to regain pre-war markets and to win new ones. The DH Dove made her first flight on 25th September 1945, followed soon after, on 10 May 1950, by the DH Heron. Both aircraft were propeller-driven unlike the revolutionary DH Comet, the world's first commercial jet

Above: A close up view of propeller building.

airliner, which became a market leader for many years.

During the heady days of the Berlin Airlift in 1948 and 1949 the Repair Department and machinists worked to wartime capacity maintaining the transport aircraft which saved West Berlin from Soviet rule.

Meanwhile, in the new West Block modest, almost Heath Robinson, experiments were being made in the new field of electronics. The types D and E Vibrators tested aircraft wings for little known inflight metal fatigue which had led to the mysterious disappearances of successful aeroplanes. By 1955 de Havilland was the largest employer in Bolton, benefiting the town with its £50,000 weekly wages bill, and by the sixties Lostock had the largest machine shop in Europe. In 1961 the electronics experiments paid off when the RAF took delivery of the DH Firestreak guided missile.

Subsequently, components were made for the Blue Streak satellite launcher rocket.

Lostock-built propellers continued to play a vital part in aeronautical development. In Operation 'Over Basseua' static aircraft were positioned to assess the effects, on equipment at varied distances, of the Christmas Island atom bomb explosions.

The Lostock site also ensured that the Short flying boats were equipped to participate in the attempted rescue of the sunken submarine HMS 'Truculent'. Following the Agadir earthquake both the DH Dove and DH Heron light aircraft were invaluable in taking supplies to local runways too damaged to support heavy freighters.

Lostock then diversified into the manufacture of air-conditioning for pressured aircraft cabins. The skilled staff turned to making mining and shoe making machinery, components for vending machines and 'Pottermeters' to measure liquid flow in pipelines, as well as aircraft under-carriages, infra-red equipment, motor car engine blocks and cigarette packing and inspection equipment. When the Lostock Supervisory Staff Association - established to forge links with a wide spectrum of commercial concerns - held an annual dinner, one guest speaker, a visitor from the National Coal Board, memorably exclaimed: 'If making space rockets and shoemaking machinery isn't playing both ends safe, I'll plait sawdust!'

Between 1937 and 1960 the Lostock branch was known as De Havilland Airscrews, except for a period during the war when it was known as DH Propellers. From 1960 to 1963 it was integrated into the De Havilland Aircraft Co, before coming under the umbrella of Hawker Siddeley Dynamics.

Above: *The factory floor covered with machinery in 1961. How noisy it must have been for these workers!* ***Below:*** *A view of the then Hawker Siddeley Dynamics factory at Lostock, which was equipped with 1,200 precision machine tools.*

In 1977 British Aerospace was formed by the merger of British Aircraft Corporation, Hawker Siddeley Aviation, Hawker Siddeley Dynamics and Scottish Aviation. This nationalised corporation survived for four years before becoming a public limited company in 1981. The company retained a clear identity throughout 50 years of complex ownership, and name changes - more particularly, the Lostock operation developed an impregnable reputation which was to stand it in excellent stead in 1989, when British Aerospace PLC became a management organisation controlling wholly owned subsidiaries. Subsequently, it was decided these subsidiary companies should market their own specialised products under their own names. So it was that Lostock became the Manufacturing Centre for the British Aerospace Dynamics Group.

A decade of dramatic change followed as the company's workforce united behind a plan to concentrate activities on the production of guided weapons systems. To this end all aspects of the business were overhauled - management structures redefined, motivational strategies improved, administrative systems revolutionised and a radical change in manufacturing philosophy adopted. The goal was to be world class, and a world-beater. Through an insistence that the company's people constituted its most valuable asset, and that teamwork and frank communication were essential at every stage, a dramatic transformation was effected at the works.

The company went into partnership in 1996 with Matra Défense of France. Under its new name, Matra BAe Dynamics, the company incorporated almost half of the French and a majority of the British missile industries. Further consolidation of the European missile industry occurred in 2001, when Matra BAe

Dynamics merged with Aerospatiale Matra Missiles of France and the Missiles Systems Division of the Anglo-Italian Alenia Marconi Systems to form MBDA. The combined company has a high-technology product range covering almost all battle scenarios - on land, at sea and in the air. It has customers in over seventy countries in five continents. With a turnover in excess of £2 billion, it has become one of the world's largest missile systems companies.

A world beater? MBDA at Lostock remains a world-class manufacturing facility at the very centre of Europe's premier missile systems company. A beacon of manufacturing excellence.

Above: *The machine shop: ALARM product line went into production in 1989.* **Below:** *MBDA Lostock, still going strong today.*

H W Audio - The Sound of Progress

Every generation has songs and sounds that evoke memories of its youth. 'Darling they're playing our tune' is not a cliché without good reason. Music and song has been part of the human experience for all of recorded history and no doubt far longer still.

Yet the story of music and singing has evolved remarkably during the lifetimes of most readers. Not least in the way that music is recorded and sold for popular consumption.

And communal enjoyment of music and song has undergone a revolution too. Sixty years ago people still gathered round the piano to sing the night away. Today, in the digital age, the pub piano has most likely been replaced by a karaoke machine, especially in Bolton.

According to television's The Big Breakfast, research showed that more karaoke discs were sold in Bolton than any other place in the United Kingdom. And who are we to argue?

Who is it in Bolton who is selling all those karaoke discs? None other than Bolton's very own HW Music Megastore, or HW Audio Ltd to give the business its official name.

Originally specialising in the sale and hire of disco equipment from the small hi-fi shop on 156 Bradshawgate, Bolton HW Music is now one of the longest established shops which were set up in the 70s disco boom. A few years after the business moved to 174 St Georges Road, with its basement being a manufacturing area for cases and speakers, the

adjoining premises were bought, doubling the sales area. A guitar and drum shop soon followed on the first floor, and soon became popular with local musicians.

The shop is the UK's largest independent music store. It stocks thousands of music-related products, from guitars, drums and basses, band and orchestral instruments, through to those karaoke discs and backing tracks for singers, music books and DVDs through to PA equipment and DJ gear and stage lighting.

The firm of HW Audio Ltd, now located at 180-198 St Georges Road, was founded in 1976.

Almost exactly a century had elapsed since sound recording had first been demonstrated. That first practical sound recording and reproduction device was the mechanical cylinder phonograph, invented by Thomas Edison in 1877 and patented in 1878.

The next major technical development was the invention of

the gramophone disc, generally credited to Emile Berliner, and commercially introduced in the United States in 1889.

Every older reader will recall the double-sided 78 rpm shellac disc which was the standard consumer music format from before the First World War until the late 1950s.

By the 1960s, however, the LP and the 45 'single' were the industry standard. In 1948, the 12" Long Play (LP) 33 1/3 rpm microgroove record album was introduced by the Columbia record company. In 1949, RCA Victor had released the first 45 RPM single. The '78 was doomed, though it would manage to survive for another ten years.

But little did the founder of HW Audio realise what other changes would be in store in more modern

Pictures: *Views of HW Audio's old 174 St Georges Road premises.*

The first premises were at 156, Bradshawgate. The fledging firm stayed for just two years before moving in 1979 to 174, St Georges Road, where Chris' brother Richard Harfield joined the firm as a 'Saturday Lad'.

At first everything sold was either homemade or produced locally by friends who had small companies. When the firm moved to St Georges Road it began to make speaker cabinets, record boxes and turntable cases in the basement. Today much is made in China and in other Far Eastern countries, but HW Audio still tries to buy British whenever possible.

times. Within just a few years the compact disc or CD, an optical disc used to store digital data, originally developed for storing digital audio, would move to the fore. The CD, introduced to the market in late 1982, remains the standard playback medium for commercial audio recordings to the present day.

But the CD was still in the future in July 1976 when Chris Harfield, then aged 23 and a graduate from Salford University, teamed up in partnership with Trevor Whiteley, a local Hi-Fi shop owner.

Before setting up the new business partnership Chris had been a disc jockey running his own disco.

The new business was originally set up with the intention of hiring out disco and public address systems to meet the ever-increasing popularity of mobile discos.

Disco events had actually already been in existence for a long time. Sir Jimmy Savile was effectively the original DJ; according to his autobiography he had been the very first person to ever use two turntables and a microphone, something which he did for the first time at the Grand Records Ball at the Guardbridge Hotel in 1947.

Twenty years later disco was booming.

At the start of the HW Audio business there was just Chris Harfield and Trevor Whiteley plus one other member of staff.

But wherever products are sourced they are certainly much more affordable than they were in the past. Prices of almost all electrical equipment have fallen dramatically down the decades: in 1976 a good, but cheap microphone was £50, today an even-better product can be bought for just £25.

Meanwhile, being in a small, specialised market the firm was susceptible to sudden downturns in trade. As a consequence it widened the product range being stocked.

Not the least of that wider range of stock was karaoke equipment and related discs.

Below: HW Audio sound & lighting flyers.

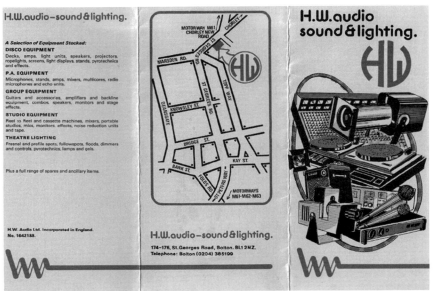

The Karaoke machine - from Japanese 'kara', 'empty', and 'okesutora', 'orchestra' - was created by the Japanese musician Daisuke Inoue in Kobe, Japan, in 1971. But tragically for him he didn't patent his invention, so missing out on becoming a multi-millionaire.

When karaoke first started to be popular in Britain, Sales Director Richard Harfield decided that this was a market that HW Audio should be in. The firm was soon making up and selling several laserdisc systems per day. The demand soon proved so great that manufacturing facilities were set up, and amplifier and mixer production began, with exports all over the world.

With the increase in business, a separate karaoke division was set up - the Karaokeshop - very efficiently run by its Manager Phil Crompton.

In 2002 HW Music moved a short distance up the road, to a building which had latterly been a car showroom, but originally was one of Bolton's cinemas. The building has been sympathetically restored, and new mezzanine floor installed. HW Music Megastore can now claim to be one of the largest independent music stores in the UK.

HW Music has always been strong on PA equipment, and the department has all that is best in PA, with all the leading makes stocked in depth.

The musical instrument department is now run by a dedicated team of three, all experienced musicians.

Installations - large and small - are undertaken throughout the country, with the firm specialising in induction loop systems for the hard of hearing.

Today the HW company not only has its thriving retail store, but also a strong internet presence with full 'e-commerce'.

Customers are not only DJs and musicians, but also a large number clients are from the educational sector.

Offering honest advice and unique back-up to its products HW Music is certainly not a here-today gone-tomorrow enterprise.

What next for HW Music? Who can say? The lesson of the last hundred years since the invention of recorded sound has been that things change with astonishing rapidity and that nothing can be taken for granted. What one can be sure of, however, is that whatever changes the future brings HW Music will be at the forefront when it comes to bringing new products to the ears of the public.

Left: HW Music Megastore, 2008.
Above: Some of HW Music staff, front seated, Richard Harfield and standing from left to right: Phil Crompton, Cameron Baxter and Marc Winstanley.

J Taylor (Electrical Contractors) Ltd - Current Affairs

If the 20th century should be called anything, that name should be 'the century of electricity'. At its start electricity was unfamiliar to most of us; by the end electrical power flowed everywhere and normal life would be impossible without it. One firm which contributed more than most to that revolution is J Taylor (Electrical Contractors) Ltd.

Around 1920 John Taylor established himself in Bolton offering electrical maintenance services to the local factories and mills. An orphan, he had been brought up at the Edgworth Children's Home and Orphange in Turton.

As electricity was becoming commonplace in the home at that time, John Taylor recognised an opportunity and his firm became one of the first to install electricity in domestic properties. In addition he set up a shop at 106 Deane Road

selling and repairing electrical appliances.

In 1930, after a short spell at gents outfitters, Scholes & Scholes, Frank Brogden, then aged 14, joined the business to begin his apprenticeship. On completion of his apprenticeship in 1938 Frank left J Taylor to join the Cunard Line as an Electrical Officer on the cruise line, sailing mainly between Liverpool and New York.

In 1939 War was declared and Frank Brogden joined the Merchant Navy.

In 1946 after surviving a torpedo attack off the coast of France, Frank returned to Bolton and to J Taylor Electrical Contractors. Frank knew that John Taylor would soon be retiring and bought the firm. Two years later the business was registered as a limited company for the first time, concentrating in industrial installations and maintenance and service contracts for the likes of Marks & Spencer, with invoices of between £1.20 and £5.00 per month.

Over the next three decades the company continued to offer electrical maintenance for the likes of Bolton Metro, schools, nursing homes and libraries etc, as well as J.W. Foster and Sons - the founders of Reebok - Kay's Foundry, Keogh Ritsons Solicitors and local engineering companies.

Mrs Brogden also worked in the shop selling lamps, electric heaters, kettles, irons, fairy lights, batteries and other electrical goods.

In 1960 the company completely rewired Hall'ith'Wood Museum, after overcoming the initial problem that some of the lads would not enter the premises - at the time it was believed to be the most haunted house in Bolton. That same year the company moved from Deane Road to Bury Road after a compulsory purchase due to intended road widening. The new location was still with shopfronted premises selling electrical goods, though with the offices at the rear.

In 1970 with the arrival of large electrical superstores such as Comet, Curry's and Dixons, the market was becoming more and more competitive. The decision was now made to close the shop and concentrate on installations and maintenance contracts. As a consequence the company relocated to Union Road.

Frank Brogden's daughter Hilary Hibbert joined the company part time in 1982 whilst her husband Jeff was abroad. In 1984, after managing a number of major petrochemical projects in Mexico and Oman, Jeff returned to the UK and took over as Director.

Over the next 25 years J Taylor (Electrical Contractors) Ltd was

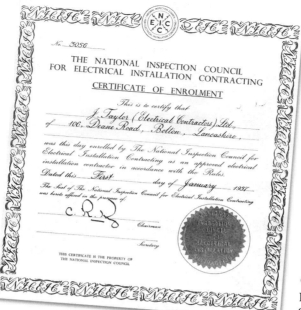

firmly established as a reliable professional and courteous company, providing high quality maintenance services and bespoke installations and electrical testing services to the local industrial and commercial sectors.

In 2000 the company moved to larger premises with offices and workshop on Tonge Moor Road. In 2007 Jeff and Hilary' son Paul Hibbert joined the company full time.

The company has continued to expand with its trusted team of qualified electricians carrying out design and installation of general power & lighting to industrial and commercial premises, school extensions for Bolton & Bury Metros and Lancashire County Council. Work has also been carried out at various production sites on Fume Cupboards and Vacuum Pump frames for export to Europe, China and the Far East.

The firm is also a specialist in flameproof wiring, working in hazardous and flameproof areas.

Since 1920 J Taylor (Electrical Contractors) Ltd has been involved with all aspects of electrical installations. Today the firm is researching micro-generation systems, solar and photovoltaic panels, wind and hydro turbines and other environmentally friendly options for next generation of electrical power in the 21st century.

Top left: Frank Brogden who after returning from the war purchased the company from John Taylor in 1946. Left: An early view of Deane Road where the company was located for over 40 years. Above: A J Taylor (Electrical Contractors) Ltd Certificate of Enrolment from 1957. Below: A staff photograph, 2008.

Russell & Russell Solicitors
Bolton's 'Helping Hand' For Over 120 Years

William Russell now launched himself into a life of public service, standing for councillor in the Church Ward, to which he was elected without opposition. At a time when great changes were afoot William was soon contributing to the Electricity, Library and General Purposes committees, helping to shape the future of the borough. In the General Election of 1922 William Russell was elected MP for Bolton with a majority of 6,000.

Less well known is that William Russell was a generous supporter of local charities; for many years he provided a three weeks seaside holiday for poor children from the proceeds of money left to him by the widow of his former employer, CW Dawson. It was said of William Russell that 'He was a man of ripe experience and his devotion to his native town was an example to be admired and followed.'

Though the firm has long since passed from the Russell family the founding principles William Russell brought to the practice are still very much in evidence.

Founded over 120 years ago, the firm of Russell & Russell Solicitors has maintained an impeccable reputation for providing first class legal advice and outstanding customer service. Known as the 'helping hand' to the people of Bolton and beyond, the firm has expanded to become one of the leading practices in the area.

In 1887 a Bolton man named William Russell started his own legal practice in the town. In 1898 he was joined in partnership by his brother Walter to form the firm Russell & Russell.

The son of George Russell, a local timber merchant, William Russell served as an articled clerk firstly under Bolton solicitor, a Mr Pennington, and subsequently with a Mr CW Dawson. The young William Russell diligently set about building his reputation for fair and sound legal dealings - a reputation which soon saw him attracting major clients such as the Bolton Union Permanent Benefit Building Society.

In 1898 William was joined by his younger brother Walter Russell – creating the partnership of Russell & Russell, the practice name which survives to the present day.

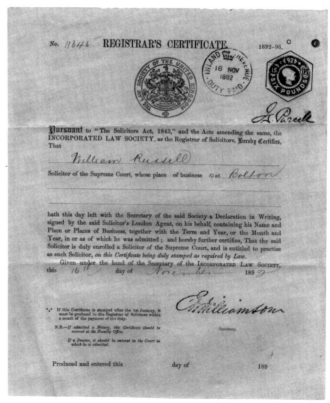

Russell & Russell aims to provide a quality service by a specialist solicitor to meet the needs of every person in almost all aspects of life whether small or large.

The firm deals with many high profile matters for both individuals and commercial enterprises. It is proud of its association with Bolton Wanderers Football Club for a number of years, during which time it secured all the licensing agreements for the Reebok Stadium.

Alan P. Walsh, who served articles at the firm prior to being admitted as a solicitor in 1975, is the current senior partner. Alan is the Managing Partner of the practice, a former President of The Bolton Incorporated Law Society, and the Deputy Coroner for Bolton, Salford, Wigan and Leigh.

Today, the practice has grown to be one of the North West's leading law firms. With nine offices, access to the best legal advice is never far away. The firm can offer help with all legal services required by the domestic or the business client.

The firm can service almost all areas of law including Conveyancing, Property Law, Licensing, Probate, Wills, Inheritance Law and services for the Elderly, Crime, Accident and Personal Injury, Matrimonial, Family and Child Care. The firm also deals with Agency Work on behalf of other solicitors and international law firms.

With its Emergency Helplines, Russell & Russell solicitors provide service 24 hours a day every day of the year.

The principal office of the firm remains in Bolton town centre in the premises known as Churchill House on Wood Street. A second Bolton office is located in Larkhill House on St. Georges Road. Branch offices are situated in Atherton, Bury, Farnworth, Horwich, Middleton and there are two associated offices in Chester.

Over 180 members of staff, including 19 partners, ensure that clients benefit from a wealth of expertise and experience across the wide range of legal services offered.

The combination of tradition and forward thinking is vital to the reputation and development of a modern law firm. Above all, Russell & Russell continues to promote the high standards that were introduced by William Russell back in 1887.

Top left: *Founder, William Russell.* **Far left:** *The Registrar's Certificate for William Russell, issued by the Law Society on the 6th November 1892. Six pounds duty was paid, as can be seen from the stamp in the top right corner.* **Above left:** *Russell & Russell's Wood Street head office.* **Left:** *Alan Walsh, Senior Partner, former President of The Bolton Incorporated Law Society, and the Deputy Coroner for Bolton.*

T Sutcliffe & Co Ltd - Concrete Progress

In 1917 during the First World War Wilfred Sutcliffe was in the Royal Flying Corps. He was injured by a propeller when starting an aeroplane engine, his arm and hand were severely injured and he was invalided home.

Wilfred Sutcliffe was a plasterer by trade; now, due to his incapacity, he started to employ other people. His first activities with four or five employees consisted of plastering, roofing and property repairs in Todmorden on the Yorkshire/Lancashire border.

In 1935 Wilfred's son Tom Sutcliffe joined the business, now based at 34 Halifax Road, Todmorden. In addition to carrying out plastering, roofing and property repairs, the firm also began selling fireplaces.

During World War II the business was mainly conducted in London and Liverpool, carrying out bomb damage repairs. The Ministry of Works commandeered the company, which was sent to the areas of heavy bombing. Tom and Wilfred were responsible for clearing bomb damage, making buildings safe and making good houses. The main office remained in Todmorden where Margaret Sutcliffe (Tom's wife) ran the business when Tom was away.

After the Second World War materials were restricted and only essential work was carried out. Eventually the firm started manufacturing and installing timber and asbestos garages, opening a show site at 81 Oxford Road, Manchester, moving to 957/959 Rochdale Road, Blackley, at the end of the 1940s. The business became T. Sutcliffe & Co. Ltd on 3rd March 1950. In 1952 Tom's son Roger Sutcliffe began working for the company at the age of 16.

After Roger's National Service, Tom and Roger diversified into the manufacture of concrete garages and buildings.

Wilfred Sutcliffe, the firm's founder, died about this time, whilst Roger's wife Ann joined the company looking after the accounts. Tom Sutcliffe died in 1963.

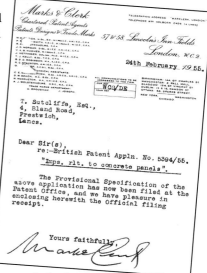

Roger continued to expand the business, opening a show site in Preston and Birkenhead and recruiting agents within a hundred mile radius.

David Ralphs became a director at this stage taking over responsibility for buying and helping to run the company. In 1971 David Ralphs suffered a heart attack and Stuart Farnell was promoted from joiner to Company Sales Manager.

Top left: *Concrete panel production in 1958.* ***Above:*** *The official filing receipt for the patent application of concrete panels, 1955.* ***Left:*** *Erecting a workshop for Naylor Bros of Skipton in 1974.*

Due to redevelopment in Manchester, the company now purchased one of Walker Tannery's in Weston Street, Bolton where it employed around 25 staff.

During the miners' strikes of the 1970s, and subsequent three day working week, the company struggled due to its heavy reliance on electricity for machinery. Manufacturing was improved by purchase of the first dry press concrete machine in

the UK in 1979, followed in 1982 by a large concrete casting machine. Aggregates were brought in from Derbyshire whilst the company tried to source as many materials as possible locally.

In 1984 a fully automated wet cast concrete plant was installed which increased quality and efficiency of pebble-dashed panel production. At this time the decision was taken to expand the business and sell garages and concrete buildings on a national scale, with agents appointed in Scotland and in the southeast of England.

In 1994 the company under Roger Sutcliffe's guidance became BS5750 quality assured - the first garage manufacturer in the country to achieve this standard.

Two years later Roger's daughter, Susan, and her husband Chris Brown, joined the firm. Chris Brown was a Chartered Quantity Surveyor and came from a construction background. He was appointed Managing Director and Susan took over from her mother to run the accounts department. David Ralphs now retired and Stuart Farnell was appointed Sales Director.

In 2005 Roger Sutcliffe retired from the company, but still has an involvement with the quality assurance audit.

The company now offers a range of small industrial buildings, pavilions, garden buildings and domestic garages. It is one of only two companies that offer a brick and stone finish, and has recently introduced anti-condensation roof sheets to the entire product range. Sutcliffe's have completed contracts for Coca Cola, Thames Barrier, Bolton Metro, Telford & Wrekin Housing, Ministry of Defence, police authorities, and continues to be involved with garage and shed replacement schemes throughout the country.

The future now depends upon continued innovation in design, and in offering a unique bespoke design service alongside a standard range of buildings. But above all Sutcliffe's believes that quality comes before quantity.

*Top: The woodworking shop in 1978. **Above left:** Founder and Chairman Roger Sutcliffe (centre) pictured with:Stuart Farnell, Sales Director (left) and Chris Brown, Managing Director (right). **Below left:** An example of a light industrial and storage building available from Sutcliffes. **Below:** One of the company's Heritage range of domestic brick finish garages.*

George Cox & Sons Ltd
A Family Tradition

In April 1947, at the age of 46, George Cox left the security of employment as a street mason with Eccles Corporation and began working for himself as 'George Cox Flagging Contractor.'

Getting work then meant going from door to door and advertising in local shops. George, who was unable to drive and could not afford to buy a vehicle, carried the flagging stones, sand, cement and tools for a day's work on his handcart and returned at the end of the day with all the waste. To his wife's dismay, their front garden in Farnworth became a storage yard and a place to park the cart. It was hard, physically-demanding work, and yet George persevered through the busy summer and autumn months with a regular supply of jobs. In the winter, he supplemented his income by carrying out roof repairs, drainage and even snow shifting.

Over the next two years George established his reputation and gained work all over Bolton. The purchase of a tipping lorry for £145 proved to be of great use but as he was still unable to drive, he persuaded a neighbour to drive it on a part time basis. George's two young sons, George Junior and Frank, would help him at weekends and during school holidays:,something that would become a family tradition.

In 1953, George Cox Senior and his two sons created their family company. George's wife, Elizabeth, was delighted when the business, now trading as George Cox & Sons, decided to move away from paths and drives - and out of her front garden - to work for local

corporations including: Bolton, Atherton, Eccles, Sale and Manchester. In 1957, the company moved into its own depot on Fletcher Street.

By 1965, the firm was employing 72 men and operating nine lorries, three vans and three cars. That year, a concrete manufacturing company, Firwood Concrete Products, was formed with the same three directors as George Cox and Sons Ltd. George Junior became Managing Director of Firwood, whilst Frank took over the running of George Cox & Sons Ltd. During this time, many notable projects were completed, not least the Walkden Memorial. This monument had stood proudly on a raised mound in the middle of the A6 for over 100 years.

Above: Founder, George Cox. **Right:** *The Walkden Memorial in its old location in the middle of the A6.* **Above right:** *The dismantling of the memorial for relocation.*

It now had to be moved to St Paul's churchyard 500 yards away. Each stone was taken down individually, numbered and lettered. Some that disintegrated during the move had to be re-cut and refitted exactly. Making the project even more memorable, a royal visitor came to town. Her Majesty the Queen, who was scheduled to visit Bolton, was to pass through the company's road works. The firm was instructed to stop work and make the site safe to allow school children to line the street as the Queen passed by.

The pedestrianisation of Victoria Square during the seventies was one of the biggest schemes the company had undertaken. The project required the closing of the road running past the Town Hall, the construction of two new water fountains and the housing of the full size beam engine wheel within a glass frame. Some 25 years on, the company also undertook the re-modelling of Victoria Square using many of the same employees who undertook the first job. Other landmark projects undertaken include Topp Way, Chorley New Road and Moss Bank Way. George Senior retired in 1970 at the age of 70 but George Cox & Sons has remained a family based company. It has come a long

way from pushcarts and cash payments. Due to the ability and dedication of George's son, Frank, the firm's reputation now extends far beyond Bolton. In the 1980s Frank's two sons, Chris and Martyn, along with his son-in-law, John Walsh, joined the firm. In 1992, with Contracts Director Geoff Absalom they took over the reigns of the company and presided over its continued growth. The company has since acquired offices in Blackburn and Stockport in addition to its Farnworth head office. The company runs 15-20 sites throughout the North West undertaking a diverse range of civil engineering projects, including roads, bridges, retaining walls, landscaping and, still, high-quality paving.

With the support of its loyal and experienced staff, delivering quality projects to its clients, this well respected family company is now set to continue for many more generations.

Top left: *The numbering and lettering of the stones for rebuilding.* ***Above:*** *The Walkden Memorial in its new location of St Paul's churchyard.* ***Below:*** *Bolton town centre, pedestrianised in 1972.*

Vernacare - Cleaner, Safer, Greener

Today 'recycling' is a very fashionable word, but actions have always spoken far louder than mere words. And some folk have been recycling not simply for years, but for decades!

More than 40 years ago local man Ken Mills, who had previously worked for a moulding company in Burscough, near Ormskirk, making packaging from paper pulp, dreamed up the concept of making disposable pulp bedpans for hospitals. Ken approached Vernon & Co in Preston, a firm which manufactured surgical dressings and was already part of the healthcare market. Impressed by Ken's idea and his experience, Vernon & Co provided the finance to set up a pulp moulding plant in Slater Street, Bolton.

The disposable pan system was embraced by the NHS and hailed as a breakthrough simply in terms of hygiene, convenience and greater acceptability to both patients and nurses. In those days 'green' still only meant a colour, not a concept.

Top: A Vernon & Co (Pulp Products) Limited certificate awarded by the Water Bylaws Advisory Service for Vernaid 750 Disposable Units. **Below and right:** *Early views of pulp packaging production.*

Ken Mills retired in the early 1970s and was succeeded as Managing Director by Mrs Jean Wilson, who had worked in the business for a number of years. Mrs Wilson was succeeded at the helm in 1997 by another long-serving employee and Bolton man Bernard Hatton, who took on the role of Chairman & Chief Executive.

The company moved to a new site on Folds Road in 1987. In 1991 the firm separated from Vernon and Co and became an independent company, Vernacare.

Today Vernacare, still based in Folds Road, provides a range of products which are a vital component in the fight against hospital-acquired infections such as MRSA and C-Difficile.

Moulded pulp remains key to Vernacare and the full range of medical pulp products is made from over-issue newspaper; grey in colour but actually they couldn't be greener. The use of recycled newspaper avoids the use of wood pulp and therefore the further harvesting of the

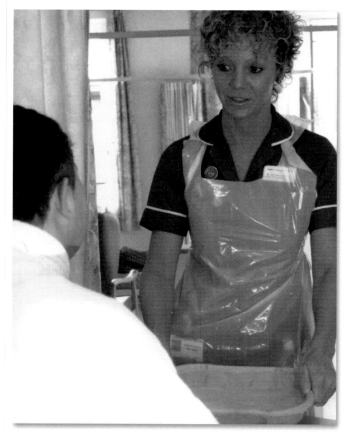

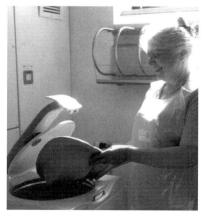

represents a major opportunity for Verna, and hospitals in South Africa are very interested in installing Vernacare products.

Over the years since its conception in the 1960s the company has bought and sold other businesses; however it is currently focussing on the core business of manufacturing infection control products, and is investing heavily in automated processing in order to improve its efficiency and retain its position as market leader.

Verna Group was privately owned until 2005 when it was bought by venture capitalists Legal & General. Following a management buyout in 2008, the business is now owned by the management team, financed by Bank of Scotland. Chief Executive Karen Haslam (another Boltonian) has been with the company for 30 years and was appointed CEO in 2005. The company has a reputation for long-serving employees, many of whom have been with the firm for over 25 years.

rainforest. The newspaper creates a natural grey colour and no bleach or dye is added, simply a waxing agent to make the products waterproof. The pulp products are 'single use' which saves nurses' time as no cleaning is required but also reduces the risk of passing on infection from re-usable plastic products.

The pulp products are disposed of by a macerator, also designed and manufactured by Verna. The maceration process is another 'green' success story for the company because these well engineered machines work on a cold water cycle, breaking down the pulp products into tiny fragments which wash away with the waste water. These machines are now used in over 80% of hospitals in the UK and exported globally.

Another division of the company, Vernatech, sells, installs and services macerators and other healthcare equipment throughout the UK. That business was started in 1991 and now has a team of over 45 with its base at the Bolton HQ, but operating throughout the UK.

The company also exports to over 43 countries worldwide and the international division offers even more opportunity for growth for the Verna Group. The firm has a subsidiary in Toronto, Canada, selling its products across North America, and as recently as 2007 set up a South African subsidiary. South Africa

*Top left: A Vernacare single-use wash bowl in use at Trafford General. **Above:** The Vernacare macerator. **Left:** Karen Haslam, Chief Executive. **Below:** An aerial view of Vernacare's Folds Road head office.*

Warburtons - 130 Years and Still Growing

It was two brothers, George and Thomas Warburton, who began the story back in 1876, when George agreed to back his brother's ambition to own a small grocery shop at 125 Blackburn Road. From these humble beginnings - and Ellen Warburton's now famed loaves and flour cakes - the business took root and has grown to become not only the country's leading independent baker but also one of the UK's biggest grocery brands.

George's son Henry joined the bakery business aged just 16. He was an intelligent and ambitious young man with an eye for an opportunity. Under the guidance of his father and Uncle Thomas, Henry learnt quickly and, by the age of 25, was a Master Baker and was completely in charge of the business. State-of-the-art machinery and new double decker ovens drove the company forward but Henry never once took his eye off product quality and personally supervised all aspects of production.

Between the late 1880s and 1915 Henry continued to expand Warburtons, moving bakeries four times in 25 years and finishing with the opening of Back o'the Bank in 1915, where Warburtons' Bolton bakery still stands today. Despite the First World War and its effects on manpower and resources, Henry worked continuously to complete his 'model bakery' that was officially opened by Rachel Warburton on July 14th that year.

The 1930s marked two momentous events in the company's development. Henry Warburton died on 5th September 1936, leaving the business to his three sons - George, Harry and Billy - while 1937 saw the arrival of the Simplex Continuous Oven.

With the arrival of the fourth generation during the late 1940s, Warburtons' appetite for expansion and development continued. The family had always believed that quality bread depended on having the very best - the best flour and ingredients, equipment and ovens. In the 50s there was a realisation that a strong team of good people to help the family build the business was also a vital ingredient. The decade saw senior personnel from outside the family joining the business, aside from Jim Aldred, the company secretary since 1936, who had been a close colleague of Harry and Billy.

Warburtons grew through acquisition of several smaller companies in the North West, including Imperial Bakeries, manufacturers of Soreen Malt Loaf - still a market-leading brand today.

Top left: *Rachel Warburton and children outside the shop in Blackburn Road.* **Below:** *The Warburtons family outside the bakery with the delivery vans and drivers.* **Above:** *Nellie Wallace the music hall star tasting the Eatmore Malt loaf in the 1930s, with Henry Warburton, his wife Rachel (left) and son George (right).*

Between 1951 and 1965, Warburtons group bread sales doubled through its five bakeries and 38 confectionery shops. During this time, in its pursuit of the best quality bread, Warburtons choose to gain control over the flour quality from its millers.

The company continued to thrive into the 70s, consolidating the great advances of the previous two decades and building new bakeries, starting with Burnley. Market changes in the late 1970s and 1980s meant that the traditional corner shop trade was losing out to the massive growth of the supermarket. Warburtons had to adapt to a new market environment and with this came the realisation that the bread needed to be marketed, something that had never been formalised before this date.

The 1990s began with the fifth generation taking the reins of the business. Expansion followed with the building of new bakeries in Nottingham, Bellshill in Scotland, and Wednesbury in the West Midlands.

Warburtons entered the 21st Century with further expansion and the opening of new bakeries in the South of the UK. In October 2003, HRH Duke of Edinburgh opened Warburtons eleventh bakery in Enfield, North London, while in 2005 the company strengthened its position in the North East, with the acquisition of a bakery in Stockton.

Warburtons largest bakery opened in 2006 at Tuscany Park, Wakefield, boasting a state-of-the-art visitor centre, which tells the story of bread making and the history of Warburtons. It was also in 2006 that Warburtons achieved full national listings with Tesco, a real milestone for the business, as it symbolised the company's transformation from a regional player to a national consumer bread brand.

In 2007, Warburtons officially opened its first bakery in Wales, marking the completion of a £10 million investment and full distribution in South Wales.

In the words of the current Chairman, Jonathan Warburton: 'I am quite sure that when Ellen and Thomas baked their first loaves back in 1876, their greatest hope would be that this new product development could help them further establish their grocery shop in Bolton. I just wonder what they would think now as we move into our 132nd year as a family business.'

Top: *A shopper in the 1950s buying her Eatmore Malt loaf at the corner shop. It was a favourite of many households from the 1930s until the late 1950s and was a testament to Warburton's marketing skills.* ***Above left:*** *Investment in new technology and state-of-the-art equipment is a vital part of Warburtons success.* ***Right:*** *Jonathan Warburton, Chairman of Warburtons.*

Thomas Harwood & Son Ltd - The Road Ahead

There's an indefinable romance which surrounds those who work in the haulage industry. Truck drivers are often referred to as 'knights of the road'. Though they often travel alone their comradeship, and willingness to help one another and other road users is the stuff of legend. That reputation is something which has grown with the modern road haulage industry, an industry which until the arrival of the first motor lorries in the first decade of the 20th century could scarcely be said to exist.

Thomas Harwood & Son Ltd, based in Francis Place, Little Lever, on the outskirts of Bolton is probably now the oldest surviving general haulage business in the area. The Harwood family line in the firm is unbroken, with Mark Harwood, grandson of the founder, now its Managing Director. Still actively involved are Mark's father Tom, his mother Joyce, and sister Diane Clow. Another sister, Elaine, previously worked for the company before moving to live in Cyprus.

The firm's founder, Thomas Harwood senior, bought his first new lorry in 1932, having begun his career in haulage with a horse and cart. It would no doubt have been a very proud moment for Thomas when he took delivery of his new truck. It was a three-ton Morris Leader, though anything up to six tons would have been loaded on it. Thomas would have been granted an A-Licence (general goods anywhere in the country) when the new Carriers' Licensing scheme was introduced as part of the 1933 Road Traffic Act.

All was not to go smoothly however. When the Morris was still quite new it caught fire whist Thomas was filling it with petrol at Bolton filling station. Happily it was able to continue in service after undergoing repairs. In the following years the business slowly expanded, and by the late 1940s the business was operating Albions, a Fordson 7V and a Commer lorry.

Thomas senior, born in 1900, died at the young age of just 49, when his son Tom was just 12. Tom's mother, Thomas Harwood's second wife, carried on the business running just two or three lorries. Alice Harwood, who would live to the grand old age of 92, now became one of a very small number of women running road haulage businesses. Though much of Britain's road

Top left: Thomas Harwood's first haulage truck, a three-ton Morris Leader. Above: Hall-Ith-Wood Lane, the site of the company's first premises. Below left: A Thomas Harwood 1960s AEC Mercury. Below: Thomas Harwood's AEC Marshal (in front of the last lorry) joins a convoy leaving Dobson & Barlow's on an export haul to Russia.

haulage industry was nationalised after the Second World War Harwood's, being a small concern, escaped that fate and so continued operating, though only with a restricted licence. That licence allowed the firm to carry washing powder from Astley Dye & Chemical Company, plus other goods, within a 25-mile radius of Bolton Town Hall - though the occasional exemption allowed for journeys as far as the Midlands. Tom Harwood joined the business as a driver and mechanic after two years National Service spent in the army where he had been a driving instructor. Earlier he had trained as a mechanic at Hopkinson's Bolton Motor Company.

In 1965 Tom became a partner in the business alongside his mother. Expansion began the following year with the purchase of the firm's first articulated lorry as well as a six-wheeler 'rigid'. Mark Harwood joined his father and mother in the firm in 1980 at the age of 18, after a short period spent working in a cotton mill. By 1990 the Harwood fleet had grown to 12 vehicles, but further expansion at its long-used Tonge Moor garage site was impossible. Tom was eventually able to buy an ideal depot at

Little Lever, which had formerly belonged to Sheldon Haworth & Wilson Transport. The move to the new depot in 1992 made further expansion possible, despite a serious economic recession which saw the end of several local clients. The firm survived only by doing what it had always done: providing the best possible customer service.

Harwood became a limited liability company in 2000.

Today the company's immaculate fleet of 17 liveried vehicles reflects the pride in a job well done over more than three quarters of a century. From its modest beginnings Thomas Harwood & Son Ltd has not only survived but prospered; that prosperity has been due to the hard work and dedication of three generations of the Harwood family, and to the invaluable support of its first class employees.

*Top left: Tom Harwood and Shep alongside one of the company's Volvo's, 1970s. **Above left:** Mark Harwood and sister Diane pictured in the yard in the 1970s. **Above:** Two of the company's new 2007 artics. **Below left:** An aerial view of the Thomas Harwood, Little Lever premises in 2007. **Below:** From left to right, Diane Clow, Joyce and Tom Harwood, Vivienne Brennand (Joyce's sister), and Mark Harwood.*

House of Raja's

'House of Raja's has become an institution' say enthusiastic visitors to our town, 'Bolton wouldn't be Bolton without it'. These days it really is hard to think of a better word to describe House of Raja's - it is indeed a local institution, a view shared by all who have visited the store. This is a great testament to the hard work of its late founder, a man who worked for over 40 years to make the firm what it is today.

On 5th May 1974, supported by a hefty bank overdraft, House of Raja's first opened its doors to the Bolton public. Back then it was simply a small family-run Asian grocery store, catering for Bolton's growing Asian population. Today the store is a landmark in the town, a cultural hotspot where customers come to learn about and experience everything concerning Indian culture, from currymaking to trying on saris. It is also the place Bolton's Asian community still relies upon to get its Indian groceries and delicacies as if they had come straight from the streets of India.

It was with the unstinting support of his father and brothers that Mr Pratap Raja and his wife Mrs Nila Raja opened up their fledgling business in Bolton's Burlington Street.

Originally trading as 'Raja's Penny Profit' the business began selling Asian groceries with Mr Raja and his wife and just two other part-time members of staff.

With his jovial nature, and his ability to make anyone try anything, from the hottest of curries to garlic paste, Pratap Raja quickly became integral to the shopping experience at Raja's Penny Profit. He was always full of hints and tips on everything from cooking to how to cure the common cold, and his customers quickly began to rely on his advice.

By 1978, as it diversified into selling traditional clothes and jewellery fronted by Mrs Nila Raja, the business had moved to Rishton Lane in Bolton. Beautiful silks and saris were shipped over from India to Bolton, often with Nila going to

a much wider audience. She worked very closely with Bolton Council and the Tourist Board to invite people from all over the North West to come and visit House of Raja's. In 2001 Sital was awarded an MBE for her services to tourism in Bolton, and she still continues to work with the Bolton Tourist Board.

Today House of Raja's is run by Nila, Sital and her husband, Pravin, with the full support of the entire Raja family (over 40 people). The business remains a unique asset to the town and a fact which is no surprise to the locals, is that the House of Raja's are even mentioned on the internet's Facebook as one of the top 50 things that make Bolton, Bolton.

India herself and choosing all the latest designs, so ensuring the people of Bolton were dressed just like the stars of Bollywood!

The business began to grow very quickly, and was soon being supported by eight full-time members of staff.

In 1982 Sital Raja-Arjan, Pratap and Nila's daughter, joined her parents in the family business. Together they decided to change the business name to 'House of Raja's' signifying the family values and strengths which underpin the way the business is run.

Now was the time for the business to think about moving to a much larger property. Mr Raja enlisted the help of his father and brother. One rainy Saturday in May the two of them were driving round Bolton looking for a property and happened to be on Fletcher Street just as a 'For Sale' sign was being put up outside number 14. Seizing the opportunity they went to the estate agent and that very same day a deal was made. The Rajas soon moved to the premises at 14 Fletcher Street where the business remains to this day.

On joining her parents in the business, Sital Raja-Arjan saw potential in the market for promoting Indian culture to

The thriving firm is a testament to the life of Pratap Raja who put his life and soul into the making the business what it is today. Now his four young grandsons are beginning to help, so ensuring that the House of Raja's will be as much an institution in Bolton's future as it is today.

Top left: Mr Pratap Raja. **Bottom left, above and below:** *Interior views of the House of Raja's.*

Gregory & Porritts
Quality and Service of Yesteryear

Buying furniture can be a tricky business. People have to live with the results for years. But at least in Bolton the process is far less tricky than in other towns.

The name of Gregory & Porritts has been synonymous with quality retailing in the town since 1895. Today the firm's Knowsley Street store is loaded from top to bottom with the most beautiful

furniture - from traditional to modern - with most of the famous names included. Nor does it end there, with the firm carrying catalogues from most manufacturers, so that what the customer sees on display in the store is only a small part of what is on offer.

Founded by two local families, the firm originally traded from Bolton Market Hall before making a move to premises in Great Moor Street in 1925.

The range of goods stocked by Gregory & Porritts was very wide, and the prices low, with a 'Penny bazaar' theme. With true Lancashire get up and go more and more goods were being added to the firm's range, and sales increased in proportion to its stock.

Despite its modest 'market stall' start the business continued to prosper, and despite the depression years, followed by the Second World War, Gregory & Porritts managed to enjoy steady growth throughout the 1930s and 1940s.

Astonishingly, despite such modest origins, by the 1940s around 60 stores in the North West were trading under the Gregory & Porritts name, including outlets in Blackpool, Chorley, Preston and even 'over the hills' in Bradford.

What has been the secret of the firm's longevity? Perhaps the store's well known slogan 'Our name is your guarantee' says it all. The firm's reputation has spread until its name has become known far and wide; today Gregory & Porritts' vans deliver as far afield as Wales, Southern England and Scotland.

It is hardly surprising that, when it comes to furnishing one's home with the finest quality at competitive prices, and with the quality of service just as high, folk are still flocking to Gregory & Porritts of Bolton after more than a century in business.

Top left: *A certificate presented to Gregory & Porritts in September 1909.* **Above:** *Store Director, John Sharples.* **Below left:** *Gregory & Porritts Knowsley Street store.* **Below:** *The new 'Exclusive Lighting' department.*

Carrs Pasties
From Tripe & Trotters to Bolton's Favourite Pasties

According to a recent poll, one of the things that makes Bolton a great place to live is Carrs Pasties. Former residents will still drive for miles just to buy a pasty, and remind themselves just how fine they taste.

The Carrs story goes back to 1939 when, with war clouds looming, Joe and Nellie Carr moved into Nellie's mother's UCP Tripe Shop on Halliwell Road, Bolton. At that time the only things sold there were tripe, cowheels, trotters (which incidentally are sheep's feet, not pig's feet as commonly thought), along with Smiths Potato Crisps, with the little blue bag of salt, and refillable soda-water siphon bottles.

When war broke out Joe Carr worked in a munitions factory and Nellie looked after the children as well as working in the tripe shop. During this time, whilst baking for the family, extra fruit pies and plain cakes were made to sell in the shop. In the early 1940s the family increased in size and moved into a house a short distance away and the shop became a 'lock-up', now with space to introduce pies and pasties to the stock in trade. As the demand for these increased basic equipment, such as a mixer and an oven, were installed.

After the war ingredients were in short supply but as time went by, and rationing was lifted, supply and demand moved up a gear. Joe and Nellie now began working full time in the shop, and the premises were bought from UCP.

During the 1940s and 1950s pasties became the most popular line. As a result 'The Tripe Shop' now became known as 'The Pasty Shop'. None of this could have been achieved without the help of Nellie's mother whose shop it had been originally.

By 1966 trade had grown and some of the children had become involved. The trade name CARRS PASTIES was now adopted.

In 1973 the Carrs Bakery was built at Manchester Road on the site of the old Railway Wagon & Iron Works.

Today Carrs Pasties sells thousands of its pasties every week to the people of Bolton and surrounding areas.

Below: *The Queen passes Carrs Pasties on her visit to Bolton in 1968.*

BIRD'S EYE VIEW

Below: How lovely it is to gaze across the rooftops on a pleasant spring morning as the trees waft gently in the breeze and we can look towards Winter Hill or Rivington Pike. Well it would be in some situations, but when Bolton was a town covered in a layer of smoke from factory chimneys and the fug created by domestic fireplaces, it was a wholly different picture. Before the various Clean Air Acts of the 1950s the air that we breathed was laden with a sooty content that blackened our buildings, left grimy deposits on our shirt collars and settled injuriously onto the lungs. With the increase in car ownership in the middle of the last century, emissions from exhausts added to the problem. When November came along, we started the annual round of peering through foggy, smoggy mornings as we set off to work or made our way to school, hankies tied across our mouths as we waited for the bus that crawled along through the gloom. Its headlights hardly penetrated the atmosphere and it is no wonder that respiratory problems kept the doctors' surgeries full.

Right: The sweeping lines of the buildings on Le Mans Crescent, so named in 1974 after the town in France with which we are twinned, are quite distinctive. Some of Bolton's most impressive and interesting architecture can be found within a stone's thrown of the Crescent. The Town Hall is a neoclassical structure, designed by William Hill who went on to work on the Portsmouth Guildhall. It was opened on 5 June 1973 by Albert Edward, Prince of Wales. The Albert Halls are incorporated within the Town Hall, the original one having burned down in 1981. It reopened in 1985 as two separate halls and several function rooms. Local stars of entertainment, including comedian Peter Kay, have put on memorable performances here in recent years. Another centre of cultural enjoyment can be seen to the left of Le Mans Crescent and the Town Hall. The Octagon Theatre, on Howell Croft North, was the first professional theatre to be built in the northwest after World War Two. It was opened by Princess Margaret on 27 November 1967.

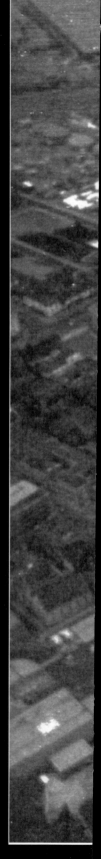

In 1934 Bolton town centre still showed evidence that the roots of its prosperity were fixed in the Industrial Revolution. Warehouses and the chimneys of factories and mills can be seen close to the railway lines that brought in the raw materials and took away the finished goods. The railway line on the left sweeps away to the north. The importance of the railway to the cotton trade can be measured by the volume of cloth that was moved in the years either side of its coming. Less than 300 million yards were being exported from Lancashire in the early 19th century but this had increased sevenfold by 1860. Bolton's first goods line opened two years earlier than that of the Manchester to Liverpool line. The Bolton to Leigh line opened in 1828. By 1840 the network system around Bolton was complete. This was well before the rest of the country and the town stole a march on others, enabling it to get off to a flying start ahead of its competitors.

The bird's eye view across the town was captured in about 1966. This was at a time when the Swinging 60s were at their peak, with mods and scooters, mini skirts and kinky boots all over the place. It was an era of fun and frivolity for many, especially the young. They knew a freedom that their parents had not experienced. The baby boomer generation did not intend to sit back quietly. It had its say and everyone had to listen as these were people with money in their pockets and they could influence both politics and the economy. It was an especially happy time on the football field. Our national side won its one and only major trophy when it lifted the World Cup at Wembley. Included in that side was Roger Hunt, a strong forward who would be transferred to Bolton from Liverpool in 1969. The photograph shows the railway lines leading into Trinity Street Station, with Newport Street, Great Moor Court and Crook Street all in view.

As the town moves forward with its plans for a massive facelift, it wants to redevelop Church Wharf with offices, homes and a multi-storey car park in a scheme anticipated to be worth between £80 million and £100 million in this area alone. So if we want to remember a spot bounded by Folds Road, St Peter's Way, Manor Street and the River Croal, we had better take note of this aerial view before a hotel, restaurants, bars, shops and an enhanced riverside walkway appear. Seen about 1966, the parish church on the left stands out clearly. This fine building was erected on the site of a 15th century predecessor, which in turn was on the site of former Saxon and Norman ones. St Peter's had fallen into some disrepair in the 19th century, but a local benefactor, Peter Ormrod (1795-1875), met the £45,000 cost out of his own money. He was a wealthy cotton manufacturer and banker, but even so this was a huge amount in mid Victorian England. James Fraser, Bishop of Manchester, officiated at the opening day consecration service on 29 June, 1871. This, as any churchgoer knows, is the feast day celebrated for both St Peter and St Paul. The church was designed by the Lancaster architect, EJ Paley, and built of Longridge stone. There is a tenor bell in the tower that dates back to 1699, though the peal of bells generally heard was only installed in 1974. The 180-feet high tower is thought to be the tallest in the county and is opened to the public on an annual basis so that, for just one day, people can gaze across the rolling countryside that is Lancashire.

ACKNOWLEDGMENTS

*The publishers would like to sincerely thank the following individuals and organisations
for their help and contribution to this publication*

Bolton Museums and Archive Service
in particular for allowing access to the Humphrey Spender's 'Worktown' photograph collection

The Bolton News

English Heritage

Halliwell Local History Society